Transformative

A Journey to a MindSet

By Steve McMahon
M. Ed. CEO MindSet Safety Management

Copyright © Steve McMahon 2025

All Rights Reserved

No part of this publication may be reproduced, distributed, or transmitted in any form or by any means, including photocopying, recording, or other electronic or mechanical methods, without the author's prior written permission, except in the case of brief quotations embodied in critical reviews and certain other non-commercial uses permitted by copyright law. For permission requests, please get in touch with the author.

Acknowledgments

A work like this emerges not from a single mind, but from countless interactions, relationships, and moments of inspiration that shape one's understanding over time. I am profoundly grateful to the many individuals who have contributed to this book in ways both seen and unseen.

This book is dedicated first and foremost to the countless parents, educators, case managers, direct care providers, organizational leaders, and all those on the frontlines who tirelessly strive each day to create nurturing, supportive, and safe environments for the students and individuals in their care. Your unwavering dedication, endless compassion, and steadfast belief in the potential within every human being serves as a powerful inspiration to us all. You are the quiet heroes whose impact echoes through generations.

I wish to express my deepest gratitude to my late mentor, Marshall Siler, whose guidance was transformative in my professional journey. Marshall's exceptional guidance fundamentally shaped my understanding of crisis management and empowered me to advocate for a more humane, empathic, and practical approach to conflict resolution. He embodied that rare combination of strength and gentleness, of unwavering principles and profound flexibility.

The wisdom he imparted—that true crisis management is about creating conditions where dignity can flourish even in the most challenging circumstances—has become the cornerstone of my approach and the foundation of this book. His legacy lives on through this work and the countless lives he touched.

To the countless students who have allowed me to share in their moments of crisis and vulnerability: your courage, resilience, and capacity for growth have taught me the most profound lessons about the human spirit. Your experiences—both the struggles and the triumphs—have shaped every page of this book.

To my colleagues who reviewed early drafts, challenged my thinking, and offered invaluable insights: your contributions have strengthened this work immeasurably. Your willingness to engage in difficult conversations and push for greater clarity and precision reflects your commitment to this field.

I am grateful to my publisher and editorial team for believing in the importance of this work and providing the guidance needed to shape these ideas into their final form.

Finally, I wish to thank my family and friends whose unwavering support, patience, and encouragement sustained me throughout this journey. You provided the stable base from which I could explore these challenging topics and the loving presence to which I could return when the work became overwhelming.

The journey of understanding transformative crisis management is one we must continue to undertake together, committed to upholding the dignity of every person involved in conflict and extending grace even in our most challenging moments.

About the Author

Steve McMahon has dedicated thirty-five years to transforming educational and organizational cultures with a focus on prevention-based approaches. Following four years of service in the United States Navy, Steve found his calling as a public school teacher, driven by his passion for nurturing children's growth and development. His diverse professional experience includes teaching students with disabilities and serving as both a program manager and district-wide behavior intervention specialist.

Steve founded Intervention Support Service in 2007, an organization dedicated to providing MindSet Instructor Certification training and consultancy services to schools and agencies. For a decade (2007-2017), he worked closely with Marshall Siler to expand MindSet training across school districts, foster care organizations, and behavioral health agencies throughout the Southeastern United States. This initiative not only equipped professionals with essential skills but also instilled a philosophy of proactive behavior management founded on intentional connections, empathy, and empowerment.

Currently, Steve serves as the CEO of MindSet Safety Management. The philosophy of this movement is built around intentional connections, empathy, and empowerment, focusing on prevention rather than reaction when dealing with challenging behaviors. In these roles, he continues to lead initiatives that provide educators and direct care providers with effective prevention strategies, creating safer and more supportive environments for all. His leadership has positively impacted numerous schools and communities across the country.

Steve and his wife, Tammy, reside in Rabun County, Georgia, nestled in the beautiful Southern Appalachian Mountains.

Foreword

In this timely and essential book, educators are invited to rethink how we approach behavior and conflict in the classroom. Drawing on research and neuroscience, Steve McMahon offers practical strategies that educators and support providers can apply immediately. He explains that navigating conflict isn't always straightforward—it requires us to stay grounded in empathy, even when emotions run high.

By helping us understand the neuroscience of conflict and trauma, develop concrete skills, build cultural awareness, and encourage an unwavering commitment to relationships, Steve shows how moments of crisis can become opportunities to build trust and connection. What makes this work particularly valuable is that it provides a practical framework for understanding complex neurobiological concepts, making cutting-edge research accessible to busy educators who need real-world applications.

Students learn best when they feel safe and supported. When classrooms are predictable and caring, students are more willing to take the risks needed for learning. Steve explains this is because feeling safe activates the prefrontal cortex—the part of the brain responsible for executive functioning essential for learning and growth, both in school and life. But the author reminds us that the reverse is also true. When students don't feel safe or question whether adults truly care about them, they are far less likely to engage in learning, especially students who have experienced trauma.

As a longtime public school teacher, I understand the complexities of classroom management. However, I must admit that I often felt unprepared to respond to crises in ways that were truly helpful. I still remember moments when a student and I both ended up feeling worse after a conflict—upset, disconnected, and unsure of what to do next. Now, as a consultant visiting schools across the U.S. and abroad, I see those same patterns happening in classrooms everywhere. That's why I hope every educator has the chance to learn from Steve's work. His strategies can help us manage crises more effectively and begin to repair the harm that trauma causes in our students' lives.

Educational leaders will find particular value in Steve's exploration of how these principles can be scaled to create organizational transformation. The same neurobiological insights that help individual teachers connect with struggling students can reshape entire school cultures when applied systematically. Leaders who understand how to create psychological safety and model empathic approaches will find their schools becoming places where both students and staff thrive.

We spend 6 to 8 hours a day with our students—we have the power to be agents of healing and change if we put these strategies into action. This book challenges us to view conflict not as something to avoid, but as an opportunity to connect more deeply and strengthen our school communities. As Steve writes, "...behind every conflict are human beings with hopes, fears, wounds, and aspirations." That includes both students and adults. If I could go back in time, I would read *Transformative Crisis Management* before my very first day in the classroom—and again at the start of every school year. I hope that you will too.

Mitch Weathers

Teacher, Organized Binder Founder, and author of Executive Functions for Every Classroom

Preface

Conflict is an inescapable part of the human experience. It arises in our personal relationships, permeates our workplaces, reverberates through our communities, and echoes on a global scale. While conflict can be unsettling, challenging, and at times deeply painful, it also presents profound opportunities for growth, learning, and the forging of stronger, more resilient relationships.

This book offers a transformative approach to conflict management one that empowers individuals to navigate the choppy waters of discord with grace, skill, and an unwavering commitment to building a more just, equitable, and harmonious world.

The path through conflict is rarely straightforward. It demands of us a willingness to embrace discomfort, to engage with perspectives that challenge our own, and to remain steadfast in our commitment to preserving the dignity of all involved—even when emotions run high and the temptation to dehumanize those who oppose us feels overwhelming.

Yet it is precisely in these moments of greatest tension that our capacity for graceful engagement matters most. When we approach conflict with an unwavering recognition of our shared humanity, we transform not only the immediate situation but also the very fabric of our communities.

As an educator and conflict resolution expert with decades of experience, I have witnessed firsthand the profound impact of conflict both in its destructive capacity and its potential to positively transform relationships. My own journey has been punctuated by experiences that have indelibly shaped my understanding of conflict and its far-reaching influence on our lives.

It is from this deeply personal perspective, intertwined with years of immersive experience in education and behavioral healthcare settings, that we have developed the MindSet Safety Management philosophy—a framework that serves as the bedrock of this book.

I recall a particularly formative experience early in my career, when I encountered a young person whose trauma history had manifested in behaviors that others found frightening and incomprehensible. Traditional approaches had failed him repeatedly, leaving both him and the staff locked in a cycle of escalation and restraint that only reinforced his deepest wounds.

It was in witnessing struggle—and the inadequate response—that I began to recognize the profound need for an approach to conflict that honors dignity above all else.

What emerged from that experience, and countless others like it, was a commitment to developing methods that would allow us to navigate crises without compromising the inherent worth of any person involved. This commitment has guided my work through decades of practice, research, and refinement. What began as an intuitive sense that there must be a better way has evolved into a comprehensive philosophy supported by emerging research in neuroscience, trauma-informed care, and practical experience across diverse settings.

In a world that often feels suffused with negativity, it is all too easy to become mired in despair, overwhelmed by the constant barrage of divisive rhetoric and the seeming intractability of the problems that plague the fabric of our society. However, this book offers a refreshing and empowering perspective that challenges us to reframe conflict in a new light.

Rather than viewing it as something to be feared, avoided, or vanquished, the MindSet philosophy invites us to embrace conflict as a catalyst for growth, learning, and the strengthening of our relational bonds. Instead of seeing conflict as an enemy to be conquered, the MindSet approach encourages us to view it with empathy, understanding, and a profound respect for the humanity of all involved.

This reframing is not merely semantic—it represents a fundamental shift in how we relate to the inevitable tensions of human interaction. When we view conflict through the lens of dignity and grace, we open ourselves to its transformative potential.

When we begin to see that the most profound moments of growth often emerge from our most challenging encounters, our capacity for empathy expands most dramatically when we engage with perspectives radically different from our own. And true reconciliation becomes possible only when we commit to preserving the dignity of everyone involved—especially those with whom we most strongly disagree.

By cultivating a culture of prevention, we have the power to transform how we perceive and navigate conflicts in both our personal and professional lives. The MindSet philosophy empowers us to proactively manage conflict rather than reactively relying on others to dictate our responses.

By taking personal responsibility and actively engaging in the process of resolution, we can approach disagreements with a sense of agency and control. This not only enables us to resolve disputes more effectively, but also allows us to grow and learn from our experiences and develop the emotional intelligence and interpersonal skills that are vital for success in all areas of life.

By embracing conflict as an opportunity for growth and engaging in the art of resolution, we can create a more harmonious and resilient society.

This preventative approach requires a fundamental reimagining of our relationship to power. Traditional conflict management often relies on power-over dynamics—the assertion of control through superior force, authority, or influence. The MindSet philosophy, in contrast, cultivates power-with dynamics: collaborative approaches that honor the agency and dignity of all stakeholders.

Throughout this book, you will encounter practical strategies grounded in this philosophy—approaches that have been tested and refined across diverse settings, from elementary school classrooms to psychiatric hospitals, from family homes to corporate boardrooms. These strategies are not merely theoretical constructs but lived practices that have transformed seemingly intractable conflicts into opportunities for profound connection.

They are offered not as rigid prescriptions but as flexible frameworks to be adapted to your unique context guided always by the twin principles of dignity and grace.

The stories shared in these pages illustrate both the challenges of conflict and the remarkable potential for transformation when we approach discord with skill, empathy, and unwavering respect for human dignity. To best illustrate the MindSet approach, I've included case studies that fall into two categories: those drawn from actual experiences in our work with students, staff, and organizations (with all identifying information removed or altered to protect privacy), and those that are composite or carefully constructed examples created to demonstrate specific aspects of our methodology. Both types serve the same essential purpose—showing how these principles translate into real-world practice and revealing the transformative potential that emerges when we prioritize connection over control.

These narratives remind us that behind every conflict are human beings with hopes, fears, wounds, and aspirations. When we honor this truth, we create the conditions for genuine resolution—not merely the cessation of hostilities, but the restoration of connection and the possibility of collective flourishing.

This book is an invaluable resource for parents, educators, mental health professionals, community leaders, and indeed anyone who seeks to navigate the inevitable conflicts of life with greater skill, understanding, and grace. Through accessible language, real-life examples, and actionable strategies, it offers a roadmap for cultivating a more peaceful and harmonious world, one interaction at a time.

With these foundational principles in mind, let us now turn to my personal journey with crisis management and the pivotal experiences that shaped the MindSet philosophy.

As you engage with the pages that follow, I invite you to approach this material not merely as information to be absorbed, but as an invitation to transformation—of your perspectives, your practices, and ultimately, your capacity to engage with conflict in ways that honor the twin pillars of dignity and grace.

For it is only when we commit ourselves to this path that we truly become agents of healing in a wounded world.

Introduction

A Personal Journey into Crisis Management

The Seeds of a Transformation

My journey in special education began with an M.Ed. from the University of West Georgia, followed by seven years as a teacher and instructional consultant in a regional specialized K-12 program. Looking back, I can see how each experience—each challenging student, each moment of connection, each difficult crisis—was gradually shaping my understanding of what truly effective intervention requires. Those early years in the classroom taught me lessons no textbook could convey.

I remember distinctly a student named Jamie (name changed for privacy), whose explosive outbursts regularly emptied classrooms and tested the limits of our traditional management approaches. Despite our best efforts, following the prescribed behavioral protocols, Jamie's behaviors only seemed to escalate. It wasn't until I abandoned the script one day—sitting quietly beside him during a meltdown instead of implementing the standard response—that I glimpsed the possibility of a different approach, one that would later align with emerging understanding of trauma responses and the importance of co-regulation in supporting dysregulated individuals. The connection forged in that moment of quiet presence accomplished what weeks of token economies and punitive consequence systems had failed to achieve.

My graduate studies had provided me with a strong theoretical foundation in understanding emotional and behavioral challenges, but it was through these years of daily work with students and staff that I began to see how theory could transform into practice. I found myself increasingly questioning the disconnect between what we knew about human development, attachment, and emerging neuroscience research, and the interventions we were implementing in our classrooms.

A Pivotal Encounter

In 1998, I had the extraordinary opportunity to attend a four-day Instructor Certification Workshop in the Prevention and Management of Aggressive Behavior. This intensive training proved to be a pivotal moment in my professional journey not only for the invaluable skills I acquired but also for the profound connections I made, particularly with Mr. Marshall Siler, the safety manager of a residential facility for adolescents.

I arrived at the training with considerable skepticism. After years of implementing various crisis management approaches, I had grown weary of techniques that promised safety but delivered only temporary compliance at the cost of meaningful relationships.

What I discovered instead was an approach that resonated with my deepest instincts about human connection and behavioral change.

When I first met Marshall, I was immediately struck by his palpable passion for helping troubled youth. During break times and after hours, our conversations extended beyond mere technique to explore the philosophy underpinning effective intervention. He spoke of creating a culture of safety rather than simply managing individual crises—a perspective that aligned perfectly with my own evolving beliefs.

Marshall quickly became not just a mentor, but a cherished friend, generously sharing insights that resonated deeply with my own developing views on effective intervention. His approach emphasized the vital importance of empathy, understanding, and proactive engagement—principles that have since become the guiding stars of my practice.

"The moment we focus more on control than connection," he would say, "we've already lost the battle."

This simple yet profound observation crystallized what I had been feeling but had struggled to articulate. Marshall's influence reinforced my steadfast commitment to creating a safe and supportive environment for both staff and students alike. I came to understand that truly effective conflict management goes beyond merely addressing disruptive behavior in the moment; it is about fostering a culture of prevention and connection that transforms the very ethos of an environment.

Confronting Uncomfortable Truths

At that time, my role as an instructional consultant encompassed supervising staff and overseeing various programs designed to support students identified as severely behavior-disordered by the local school systems. Our program was considered effective by conventional standards—incidents were documented, protocols were followed, and some students eventually returned to less restrictive environments. Yet beneath these metrics of success, I harbored a growing discomfort with our methods.

Our previous approach, while functional for some students, failed to truly address the complex—and at times hostile—relationships we inadvertently developed with them. We relied heavily on physical restraint, believing it was necessary to ensure safety, but as I reflected on these incidents, I could not shake the deep discomfort that accompanied these actions.

I vividly recall one incident that forced me to confront the limitations of our approach. A thirteen-year-old student—a survivor of severe early childhood trauma—was physically restrained after throwing a chair in the classroom. Though the restraint was performed exactly according to protocol, I couldn't ignore the look of betrayal in his eyes. In that moment, I realized that while we had controlled the immediate situation, we had damaged something far more precious: the fragile trust this young person had begun to develop in adults who claimed to care for him.

We sequestered students in time-out rooms, hoping isolation would allow them to calm down, but these practices were more punitive than supportive—more about enforcing compliance than cultivating connection. The unsettling realization that we were prioritizing control over understanding haunted me. Each incident left me questioning whether we were truly addressing the underlying issues or merely suppressing behavior in the moment through the looming threat of punishment.

Despite our best efforts, we could not seem to escape the constant undercurrent of tension and conflict that arose between us and the students. It became increasingly clear that our methods were failing to address the root causes of their behavior. We needed a better way—a more humane, empathic, and proactive approach that prioritized understanding and connection over control and punishment.

The Birth of a New Approach

The weeks following the PMAB workshop were transformative. Armed with new insights and techniques, I began implementing changes in our program—not just in crisis response protocols, but in the fundamental way we approached our relationships with students. This shift was particularly timely, as the 1997 reauthorization of the Individuals with Disabilities Education Act (IDEA) had introduced new requirements for addressing challenging behaviors, including the mandate for Functional Behavioral Assessments (FBAs) and Behavior Intervention Plans (BIPs) for students whose behavior impeded their learning or that of others (Yell & Katsiyannis, 2000). What had once been considered optional best practice was now federal requirement, mandating that schools look deeper into the functions and meanings behind problematic behaviors.

We shifted from a focus on consequences to an emphasis on prevention and connection, a change that aligned with emerging research on positive behavioral supports and school-wide approaches to behavior management (Sugai & Horner, 2002). Staff meetings moved beyond discussing behavior incidents to exploring the unmet needs these behaviors might be communicating—exactly what the new FBA requirements demanded. This legislative framework provided both validation and structure for our transformation.

This transition wasn't easy. Many team members had been trained in traditional behavior management approaches and were initially skeptical of what seemed like a "softer" approach, even though evidence-based practices were now legally required. Change required not just new techniques but a fundamental shift in perspective—seeing challenging behaviors not as deliberate defiance, but as communication from young people lacking better tools to express their needs.

Over time, however, the results spoke for themselves. Physical restraints decreased. Staff turnover, previously a chronic challenge, stabilized as team members reported greater job satisfaction and reduced burnout. Most importantly, our students began to thrive in an environment characterized by genuine care rather than controlled compliance. What had begun as intuitive adjustments evolved into a systematic framework for creating safe, supportive environments for both students and staff.

Expanding the Vision

As word of our program's transformation spread, I received increasing requests to share our approach with other schools and facilities. What began as informal presentations to local institutions gradually expanded into structured training programs. I found myself increasingly drawn to this work of equipping others with tools to create safer, more empathic environments.

In 2002, my role in the school district shifted from program manager to district-wide Behavior Intervention Teacher. This role provided access and opportunity to broaden the scope of the MindSet approach and deliver professional development within the context of the K-12 general education setting across our very large school district.

What started with two professional educators in 2002 quickly grew to a team of five. These new roles aligned well with educational reform movements that were emerging during this period. The 2004 reauthorization of IDEA introduced Response to Intervention (RTI) as an alternative approach to identifying students with learning disabilities, emphasizing early intervention and data-driven decision making. While RTI initially focused primarily on academic interventions, it laid important groundwork for what would later evolve into Multi-Tiered Systems of Support (MTSS)—a comprehensive framework that integrates academic and behavioral supports. The preventative focus and tiered intervention model of what would become MTSS aligned perfectly with our team's mission and the growing recognition that effective education required addressing both academic and behavioral needs proactively.

In 2007, I founded Intervention Support Service, LLC, as a part-time venture while continuing my work with the school district, dedicated to spreading these transformative approaches beyond our local context. As the need for our program increased and requests for training grew, I was able to transition to this movement full-time in 2011. Those early years were challenging—building credibility, refining our training methodology, and balancing the demands of a growing program. Yet the work itself was profoundly rewarding, as we witnessed one institution after another experience the same transformation we had seen in our original program.

Today, as CEO and Director of MindSet Safety Management, I have the privilege of sharing these transformative approaches with educational institutions and community behavioral health providers across the country. Our team has trained thousands of professionals from classroom teachers to residential care staff to hospital personnel—all united by a commitment to creating environments where safety derives from connection rather than control.

Looking Forward

The publication of this book represents the next phase in this journey—an opportunity to share our approach with an even wider audience. The pages that follow distill two decades of experience, research, and refinement into a comprehensive framework for transformative crisis management. From the foundations of trauma-informed practice to practical de-escalation techniques, from building organizational culture to sustaining meaningful change, each chapter builds upon the core belief that has guided my work from the beginning: that creating truly safe environments requires genuine connection, not merely effective control.

As you read, I invite you to bring your own experiences and insights into dialogue with these ideas. Whether you're an educator, mental health professional, healthcare worker, or leader seeking to create positive change in your organization, my hope is that you'll find both practical tools and inspirational vision for your own journey.

The work of transforming crisis management is far from complete. New challenges emerge as our understanding of human behavior and development evolves. The contexts in which we apply these principles continue to diversify. Yet the fundamental truth remains constant: when we prioritize connection over control, when we respond to challenging behavior with curiosity rather than judgment, when we create environments characterized by both accountability and compassion, we unlock the potential for profound and lasting change—both in the individuals we serve and in ourselves as practitioners.

This book is both a roadmap and an invitation—to join a growing community of professionals committed to reimagining crisis management as an opportunity for healing, growth, and transformation. The journey continues, and there is always room for more voices, more insights, and more hands in this essential work.

References

Sugai, G., & Horner, R. H. (2002). The evolution of discipline practices: School-wide positive behavior supports. *Child and Family Behavior Therapy, 24*(1-2), 23-50.

Yell, M. L., & Katsiyannis, A. (2000). Functional behavioral assessment and IDEA '97: Legal and practice considerations. Preventing School Failure, 44(4), 158-162.

Chapter 1: The Neurobiology of Crisis Response

To truly transform how we respond to crisis, we must first understand what happens beneath the surface when humans encounter threat or overwhelming stress. This chapter explores the remarkable neurobiological systems that govern our responses to crisis—knowledge that forms the foundation for everything that follows in our journey toward transformative crisis management.

When we encounter people in crisis, whether in schools, treatment centers, or community settings, what we see on the surface often tells only part of the story. Beneath visible behavior lies a complex interplay of neurobiological systems shaped by millions of years of evolution. Recent advances in neuroscience have revolutionized our understanding of human behavior, particularly during times of stress and conflict.

Our approach begins with a fundamental premise: human behavior during a crisis isn't simply a matter of conscious choice, but rather emerges from sophisticated brain systems designed to keep us safe and connected. By understanding these systems, we can develop more effective, compassionate approaches to supporting people through difficult moments.

The Brain's Role in Crisis Response

The human brain is a marvel of evolutionary engineering. While we often focus on the thinking, reasoning functions of the cerebral cortex, equally important are the subcortical region structures beneath the cortex that regulate our most essential functions and responses (LeDoux & Pine, 2016). These regions operate largely outside our conscious awareness yet profoundly influence how we perceive and react to our environment.

Key brain regions involved in crisis response include the amygdala, which rapidly detects potential threats and triggers protective responses, the hypothalamus, which coordinates stress hormones and basic drives, the brainstem, which governs vital functions and basic arousal states, and the limbic system, which processes emotions and attaches significance to experiences.

Together, these structures form what neuroscientists call our "surveillance system"—an intricate network continuously scanning our environment for signs of safety or danger. This scanning happens automatically, before our conscious mind has time to process what's happening.

Understanding the Three-Circuit Response System

Polyvagal Theory, developed by Dr. Stephen Porges, provides a valuable framework for understanding how our nervous system responds to different environmental conditions. This theory describes three distinct neural circuits that evolved to help humans navigate varying levels of safety and threat (Porges, 2011). While this theory has generated scientific debate and some of its specific claims remain contested by researchers, it offers a useful clinical framework for understanding different states of nervous system activation.

The Social Engagement System: Our Connection Circuit

When our environment signals safety, our most evolutionarily advanced circuit activates. This system, according to polyvagal theory, is regulated by the ventral vagal branch of the vagus nerve and represents our newest and most sophisticated survival strategy. In this state, we experience calm, regulated physiological states with optimal heart rate variability, rich facial expressiveness and melodic vocal prosody, enhanced capacity for attentive listening and genuine engagement, full access to complex thinking and creative problem-solving, natural ability to form and maintain meaningful social connections, and integration between our emotional and rational brain centers.

This state creates optimal conditions for learning, growth, and relationship building. Most importantly, it allows complete access to our prefrontal cortex—the brain region responsible for planning, decision-making, empathy, and our highest human capacities. People in this state appear warm, present, and genuinely available for connection.

The Mobilization System: Our Protection Circuit

When our nervous system detects potential threat, our sympathetic nervous system rapidly activates. This "fight-or-flight" response evolved to protect us from physical danger but also triggers during social threats, work stress, or perceived rejection. This mobilized state involves significantly increased heart rate, blood pressure, and respiratory rate, heightened alertness and hypervigilance scanning for danger, muscle tension and physical preparation for defensive action, narrowed attentional focus on immediate survival needs, reduced capacity for complex thinking and nuanced perspective-taking, and decreased access to empathy and social connection abilities.

Understanding this state helps explain why logical interventions often fail during crisis moments. When someone's brain operates in protection mode, their biology prioritizes immediate survival over learning, connection, or rational discourse. The person may appear agitated, argumentative, or unable to "hear" reasonable suggestions—their nervous system has shifted priorities entirely.

The Immobilization System: Our Shutdown Circuit

When our nervous system perceives life-threatening danger with no possibility of escape or successful defense, the most ancient circuit assumes control. According to polyvagal theory, this system is regulated by the dorsal vagal branch of the vagus nerve and represents our oldest survival strategy, essentially "playing dead" when other options fail. This state involves dramatic slowing of heart rate and metabolic processes, significantly decreased muscle tone and energy conservation, disconnection from present-moment awareness and surroundings, profound numbing of physical and emotional sensations, overwhelming sense of helplessness, hopelessness, or "going blank," and dissociation from thoughts, feelings, and bodily awareness.

People in this shutdown state often describe feeling "frozen," "empty," "not really there," or like they're "watching life from outside themselves." They may appear calm or compliant on the surface but internally experience profound disconnection from themselves and others. This state commonly manifests as depression, chronic fatigue, dissociation, emotional numbness, or complete withdrawal from social engagement.

Understanding this circuit illuminates why some individuals "shut down" rather than become agitated during overwhelming stress. It also explains why encouraging someone to "snap out of it" or "think positive" proves ineffective—their nervous system has essentially gone offline as protection from perceived annihilation. Recovery requires gentle, patient re-engagement with consistent safety cues rather than direct confrontation or forced activation.

Beyond Fight, Flight, and Freeze: Flock and Fawn Responses

While fight, flight, and freeze responses are widely recognized, recent trauma research has expanded our understanding to include two additional defensive adaptations: the flock and fawn responses.

The Flock Response: Seeking Safety in Numbers

The "flock" response describes the instinct to seek safety through connection with others in the face of threat. Unlike the individualistic fight-flight responses, flocking represents a collective survival strategy observed across many social species. This response leverages features of the social engagement system, but with a defensive rather than a purely social purpose. It represents an adaptive hybrid that uses connection as a protective mechanism.

The neurobiological basis of flocking involves both the social engagement system and specific fear-processing pathways. Research has documented that individuals under stress may exhibit a "tend-and-befriend" pattern that promotes caregiving and social affiliation under conditions of threat.

In crisis situations, individuals exhibiting a flock response may instinctively seek proximity to trusted others when threatened, feel dramatically safer in the presence of specific attachment figures, demonstrate enhanced capacity to regulate when in supportive groups, show increased distress when isolated from supportive connections, and use affiliation as their primary strategy for managing threat.

The Fawn Response: Appeasing to Survive

The "fawn" response describes a survival strategy characterized by appeasing behaviors, people-pleasing, and emotional attunement to perceived threats. This response is particularly common in children who experience relational trauma with caregivers. When fight, flight, and freeze are not viable options—as is often the case for dependent children—the nervous system may default to fawning behaviors as the only available survival strategy.

Neurobiologically, the fawn response represents a complex interaction between the social engagement system and defense mechanisms. It employs the neural circuitry designed for connection but redirects it toward safety rather than authentic relationship. Children who develop this response learn to track subtle cues of others' emotional states with hypervigilant accuracy, while simultaneously suppressing awareness of their own needs and feelings (Schore, 2003).

In crisis situations, individuals with dominant fawn responses may become excessively compliant when threatened, automatically prioritize others' needs while neglecting self-protection, display remarkable attunement to others' emotional states, struggle to identify and express their own needs, and experience internal distress while presenting as calm and helpful.

Because fawning can look like cooperative behavior, it's frequently misinterpreted as a sign of safety and connection rather than what it actually is—a sophisticated survival strategy. Practitioners who miss this distinction may inadvertently reinforce the pattern by praising the compliance without recognizing the underlying autonomic distress.

Clinical Examples of Crisis Responses

The Fight Response in Action

During a team meeting at a community mental health center, Andrew, a 34-year-old case manager, suddenly slammed his hand on the conference table when his supervisor announced new documentation requirements. "This is ridiculous!" he shouted, his face flushed red. "We're already drowning in paperwork, and now you want us to do more? When are we supposed to actually help people?"

His voice rose with each word, his body leaning forward aggressively toward his supervisor. Other team members shifted uncomfortably in their chairs as Andrew continued, his breathing rapid and shallow. "You have no idea what it's like on the ground. You just pile on more bureaucracy while we're trying to keep people alive!"

This was Andrew's fight response in full activation—his sympathetic nervous system had detected the new requirements as a threat to his ability to do meaningful work, triggering an immediate impulse to confront and challenge. The fight response is driven by a biological imperative to defend against perceived threats through confrontation, with the nervous system prioritizing survival over social appropriateness.

Understanding the fight response, Andrew's supervisor took a different approach than immediate disciplinary action. She recognized that his outburst, while inappropriate in delivery, contained important information about systemic stress and workload concerns. Instead of escalating with authority, she acknowledged his distress: "Andrew, I can see you're really frustrated about the additional requirements. Your concern about having time to help clients is exactly the kind of feedback we need to hear."

She validated his underlying concerns without endorsing his aggressive delivery: "The tension between documentation requirements and direct service time is real, and it makes sense that you'd feel upset about anything that seems to take away from client care." Finally, she empowered him to be part of the solution: "What ideas do you have about how we might streamline these requirements while still meeting our compliance needs?"

This approach recognized that Andrew's fight response wasn't simply disrespectful behavior, but a passionate defense of his values and purpose. By addressing the underlying concerns while maintaining appropriate boundaries about communication style, his supervisor created an opportunity for productive dialogue rather than disciplinary consequences.

The Flight Response in Action

During a mandatory individual counseling session at an outpatient treatment center, Emma, a 26-year-old in early recovery, suddenly stood up. Before the therapist could say a word, she was moving toward the office door, her eyes darting around the room, avoiding eye contact. "Emma, we need to discuss your treatment plan," the therapist called, but Emma was already halfway to the door.

This was Emma's flight response in full activation. Her sympathetic nervous system had detected the counseling session as a threat, triggering an immediate impulse to escape. The flight response is driven by a biological imperative to move away from perceived danger, with the nervous system prioritizing survival over compliance.

The therapist recalled the principles of supporting flight responses. Instead of blocking Emma's path or escalating the situation with demands, she spoke in short, clear sentences, kept her body language open and non-threatening, provided a clear exit path, reduced environmental stimulation, and offered controlled movement options. "Emma," she said calmly, "I see you're feeling overwhelmed. Would you like to take a short walk in the hallway and do some breathing exercises? We can continue our discussion when you feel more comfortable."

Her approach recognized that Emma's flight response wasn't deliberate misbehavior, but a sophisticated survival strategy. By offering a regulated way to address her need to move and create distance, she created an opportunity for Emma to return to a more regulated state.

The Freeze Response in Action

During a morning check-in at an addiction recovery residential program, Nathan became completely still when asked about his recent challenges. He became motionless, his eyes unfocused, barely breathing. This was Nathan's immobilization response—a neurobiological survival strategy when fight or flight feels impossible. It wasn't resistance or stubbornness, but a deep biological protection mechanism.

Understanding appropriate engagement approaches, the recovery counselor first focused on regulation. She spoke softly, created a calm environment, and offered a soft, weighted blanket. She didn't demand responses or push for interaction. "I'm here," she said quietly. "You're safe." Gradually, she offered simple, rhythmic activities—sorting cards, gentle breathing exercises—that could help Nathan's nervous system feel more secure without overwhelming him.

The Flock Response in Elder Care

When George's usual companion was absent during the morning social hour at an assisted living community, he became visibly anxious. He kept looking around the room, seeming unable to engage with others. This illustrated the flock response—George's nervous system seeking connection as a primary regulatory strategy. Rather than seeing this as dependency, the community coordinator recognized it as a valid biological adaptation.

She helped George create a symbolic connection, giving him a framed photo of his companion and allowing brief video calls. She also ensured he had proximity to other trusted residents, understanding that social connection was a crucial regulatory tool for him.

The Fawn Response in Educational Settings

During a class discussion about a recent field trip, Ms. Carter noticed Kai seemed different. When called on, he immediately began agreeing with everything she said, his eyes darting nervously around the room. "Did you enjoy the museum, Kai?" Ms. Carter asked. "Oh, yes! Whatever everyone else thought," Kai responded, his voice slightly high-pitched and eager to please.

This was Kai's fawn response in action, a survival strategy learned from past experiences where appeasing others felt safer than expressing his authentic self. Fawning is a sophisticated adaptation where a person prioritizes the perceived safety of others by mirroring their wishes while suppressing their own needs.

Ms. Carter gently responded, "I'm curious about your actual experience. What did you find interesting about the museum?" By creating space for Kai's authentic voice, she helped him develop a sense of safety in expressing his true thoughts.

Recognizing Response Patterns

Understanding these five response patterns—fight, flight, freeze, flock, and fawn—expands our framework for crisis intervention. This nuanced approach helps us recognize that what may appear as adaptive social behavior (flocking or fawning) might actually represent sophisticated defensive adaptations requiring specific support for the underlying autonomic distress.

Recognizing all five response patterns allows crisis responders to better identify and address the full spectrum of survival adaptations they may encounter. Rather than interpreting behaviors through the lens of compliance or defiance, we can understand them as neurobiological adaptations that served important protective functions.

Conclusion

Understanding the neurobiology of crisis response provides a foundational understanding that transforms how we interpret and respond to challenging behaviors. By recognizing that our reactions during moments of stress stem from sophisticated brain systems designed for survival, we move from judgment to curiosity, from control to understanding.

This neurobiological framework encompassing the three-circuit response system and the five defensive adaptations—gives us a precise language for understanding human behavior during crisis. When we recognize that the amygdala's threat detection, the sympathetic nervous system's mobilization, or the dorsal vagal system's shutdown are automatic protective responses rather than conscious choices, we create space for more effective, compassionate intervention.

These neurobiological insights become the foundation for the MindSet Four-Step Model we'll explore in detail in Chapter 6—a systematic approach that works with rather than against the nervous system's protective wisdom.

Understanding crisis responses through nervous system activation levels

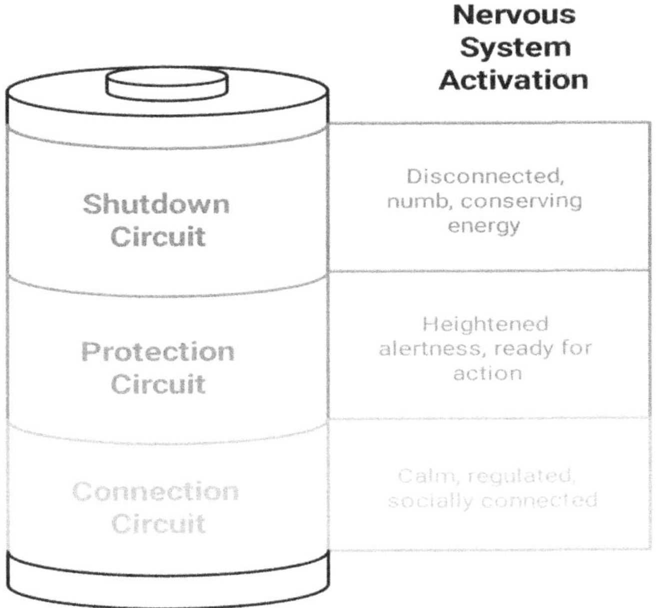

Questions for Personal Reflection or Group Discussion

Consider these questions individually or discuss with colleagues to deepen your understanding of how neurobiological principles apply to your practice.

Understanding Your Own Responses

1. **Self-Awareness in Crisis Moments** Think of a recent situation where you felt triggered or reactive. Looking back through the lens of the three-circuit response system, which nervous system state were you likely experiencing? What early warning signs could you learn to recognize in yourself?
2. **Recognizing Defense Patterns** Consider the five response patterns described in this chapter (fight, flight, freeze, flock, fawn). Which pattern do you most often default to when feeling stressed or threatened? How might this awareness change how you approach challenging situations?

Application to Your Practice

3. **Reframing Challenging Behaviors** Think of someone in your care whose behavior you find particularly challenging. How

might understanding their behavior as a neurobiological adaptation rather than a conscious choice change your response? What survival function might their behavior have served?

4. **Creating Safety Cues** Given what you now understand about neuroception and the continuous scanning for safety or threat, what specific changes could you make to your environment, body language, or communication style to signal safety to those you serve?

Systemic Reflection

5. **Organizational Implications** How might the neurobiological principles in this chapter inform policies and practices in your organization? What current approaches might inadvertently trigger defensive responses, and how could they be modified to support nervous system regulation?

Integration Practice: Over the next week, observe one interaction each day through the neurobiological lens presented in this chapter. Notice what you see differently when you understand behavior as communication from the nervous system rather than as choice or defiance.

References

Janak, P. H., & Tye, K. M. (2015). From circuits to behaviour in the amygdala. Nature, 517(7534), 284-292.

LeDoux, J. E., & Pine, D. S. (2016). Using neuroscience to help understand fear and anxiety: A two-system framework. American Journal of Psychiatry, 173(11), 1083-1093.

Perry, B. D. (2009). Examining child maltreatment through a neurodevelopmental lens: Clinical applications of the neurosequential model of therapeutics. Journal of Loss and Trauma, 14(4), 240-255.

Porges, S. W. (2011). The polyvagal theory: Neurophysiological foundations of emotions, attachment, communication, and self-regulation. W. W. Norton & Company.

Schore, A. N. (2003). Affect dysregulation and disorders of the self. W. W. Norton & Company.

Chapter 2: Transformative Crisis Intervention in Practice

Armed with understanding how the nervous system responds to crisis, we now turn to the practical question: How do we translate neurobiological insights into real-world intervention strategies? This chapter demonstrates how to move from reactive crisis management to transformative approaches that honor human dignity while creating genuine safety.

Understanding the neurobiology of crisis response creates the foundation for effective intervention, but knowledge alone doesn't transform practice. This chapter bridges the gap between neurobiological understanding and practical application, demonstrating how to translate insights about nervous system functioning into real-world crisis response strategies.

We'll explore the fundamental difference between transactional and transformative approaches to crisis intervention, examine detailed case examples, and provide concrete strategies for supporting nervous system regulation during challenging moments. The goal is not simply to stop unwanted behaviors, but to create conditions where genuine healing and growth can occur.

A Middle School Crisis: Two Approaches in Action

The Classroom Eruption: A Double Activation

Erica stared at the math test on her desk, the red "D" seeming to pulse with each heartbeat. Her shoulders tensed as Mr. Rivera approached, already frustrated from an earlier confrontation with another student. "I see you're still struggling, Erica," Mr. Rivera said, his voice sharp and carrying across the classroom. "Maybe if you paid more attention instead of daydreaming, we'd see some improvement." Mr. Rivera's jaw was tight, his posture rigid—signs of his own sympathetic nervous system activation, though he wasn't aware of it.

Something inside Erica snapped. She shoved the test off her desk and stood abruptly, knocking her chair backward with a crash that silenced the room. "Shut up talking to me!" she shouted, her face flushed, fists clenched at her sides. "You never help me! You just wait for me to mess up!"

Mr. Rivera, now fully triggered himself, stepped closer with his own defensive posture. His face reddened and voice raised, "Sit down right now, young lady!" he commanded, pointing forcefully at the chair. "This behavior is completely unacceptable!" His quickened breathing and increased volume revealed his own fight response activating.

Erica backed away, bumping into desks. Her breathing was rapid and shallow, eyes darting between Mr. Rivera and the door. "You don't care if I get it," she said, her voice breaking. "You don't even know me!" The two stood locked in a classic threat cycle—each one's defensive response triggering and intensifying the other's, creating an escalating loop of reactivity.

The Transformative Intervention

Ms. Jackson, a paraprofessional from the classroom across the hall, heard the commotion. She had recently completed de-escalation training and recognized what was happening when she glanced through the door window. She could see that both Erica and Mr. Rivera were in protection mode, their nervous systems shifted into sympathetic activation. Neither had access to their rational thinking in this moment.

She entered quietly and moved to the side of the room, making herself visible but non-threatening. "Erica," she said calmly, her voice low and even. "I can see you are really upset right now. Would you like to take a short break with me in the hallway?" Erica looked at her, still breathing hard, but some of the tension in her shoulders eased slightly at the sight of Ms. Jackson, who had built a positive rapport with her during lunchtime conversations about the local professional baseball team.

"Yes," Erica managed, her voice still tight with emotion. Ms. Jackson briefly turned to Mr. Rivera. "Mr. Rivera, I'll work with Erica in the hallway. I'll check back with you shortly." Mr. Rivera nodded stiffly, visibly trying to contain his own reaction as he stepped back to create space.

The Art of Co-Regulation: Working with Erica

In the hallway, Ms. Jackson didn't demand explanations or issue consequences. Instead, she guided Erica through several deep breaths and simple grounding exercises, demonstrating the power of co-regulation—using her own regulated nervous system to help stabilize another's. "Feel your feet on the floor... notice the colors in the hallway... take another breath with me," Ms. Jackson instructed gently.

Only after Erica's breathing slowed and her fists unclenched did she begin a conversation. "That must have been really hard." This represents the Acceptance step of what will become our four-step framework. Erica looked up and said, "Yeah, he has no idea." At that moment the two shared a pivotal connection.

Ms. Jackson continued, "That happens to us when we feel threatened or overwhelmed." This demonstrates the Validation step—normalizing the response. Erica nodded, the biology-based explanation offering dignity rather than shame for her reaction. "I just get pissed when I try hard and still fail," she admitted. "And then Mr. Rivera points it out in front of everyone."

Ms. Jackson replied with an understanding tone and simply asked, "So what do you need right now that might help you calm down?" This exemplifies the Empowerment step—offering meaningful choice.

Supporting Adult Regulation: Working with Mr. Rivera

Ms. Jackson returned to Mr. Rivera's classroom after ensuring Erica was settled. The rest of his class was working on an assignment, and he stood near his desk, still looking tense but more composed than before. "Do you have a moment to talk about what happened?" Ms. Jackson asked quietly.

Mr. Rivera sighed, running a hand through his hair. "I shouldn't have spoken to her that way," he admitted. "It's been a tough day, but that's no excuse." Ms. Jackson nodded, her posture open and non-judgmental. "When we're already stressed, it's much harder to respond skillfully to challenging situations. What happened today involves normal brain functioning under stress."

"She disrespected me in front of the whole class," Mr. Rivera explained. "In that moment, all I could think about was putting her in her place. I let her get under my skin." "That's your brain's protective circuit activating," Ms. Jackson explained. "When we perceive a social threat like disrespect, especially in front of others, our nervous system responds just as it would to a physical threat. Your reaction wasn't a character flaw—it was your brain trying to keep you safe."

Mr. Rivera's shoulders relaxed slightly. "I've been working with Erica all year, trying different approaches. Nothing seems to help her engage with the material. Then when she fails a test, this happens." "What do you think might help repair the relationship with Erica?" Ms. Jackson asked.

Mr. Rivera thought for a moment. "I need to acknowledge how I contributed to the situation. And maybe find a different way to support her learning that doesn't set off this cycle." "Would you be open to a brief conversation with Erica later today, after you've both had time to process?" Ms. Jackson suggested. "I'd be happy to facilitate." Mr. Rivera nodded. "Yes, I think that would be helpful."

The Restorative Conversation: Creating New Patterns

Later that afternoon, after both had fully regulated, Ms. Jackson brought Erica and Mr. Rivera together in a small conference room. Though not a counselor, her recent training had equipped her with skills to help mediate such situations. "Thank you both for being willing to have this conversation," Ms. Jackson began. "What happened today is actually very normal brain functioning. When we feel threatened, our thinking brain goes offline and our survival brain takes over. Erica, your brain detected criticism as a threat. Mr. Rivera, your brain registered defiance as disrespect, another kind of threat."

She continued, "I'm wondering if each of you might be willing to share what was happening for you during that moment, and what you might need going forward." Erica spoke first, hesitantly. "I studied for that test, but I still didn't get it. Then when you called me out in front of everyone..." she trailed off, looking down.

Mr. Rivera nodded thoughtfully. "I didn't realize you had studied. I misinterpreted your struggles as lack of effort, and I responded in a way that made things worse. I'm sorry about that." "Math just doesn't make

sense to me sometimes," Erica admitted. "And then I feel stupid."
"You're not stupid," Mr. Rivera said firmly. "Different brains process information differently. Maybe we need to find another approach that works better for how you learn."

Ms. Jackson facilitated as they developed a plan: Mr. Rivera would provide feedback privately rather than in front of the class, Erica would signal when she was feeling overwhelmed with a simple hand gesture, and they would meet weekly to review concepts using alternative teaching methods.

"If you're both comfortable with this plan, I think it gives us a good foundation to build on," Ms. Jackson said. "Remember, what happened today wasn't about either of you being 'bad' or 'wrong'—it was about two nervous systems getting caught in a threat cycle. With practice and these new strategies, you can create a different pattern."

This framing allowed both teacher and student to understand their interaction through a neurobiological lens rather than as character flaws or intentional disrespect. Together, they identified triggers and strategies to recognize and interrupt future escalation cycles before they spiraled out of control.

Three Months Later: Building on Success

The true measure of transformative crisis intervention lies not in single moments of connection, but in how those moments create lasting change in relationships and systems. Three months after their initial conflict and restorative conversation, the relationship between Erica, Mr. Rivera, and

Ms. Jackson had evolved in ways that demonstrated the long-term impact of their neurobiologically-informed approach.

Sustainable Relationship Changes

Mr. Rivera had internalized the lesson that Erica's struggles weren't about defiance but about genuine learning challenges combined with emotional overwhelm. He began recognizing early warning signs—the slight tension in her shoulders, the way she gripped her pencil more tightly, the subtle change in her breathing when material became frustrating.

"I watch for her stress signals now," Mr. Rivera explained to a colleague. "When I see them, I'll quietly check in or offer a different approach before things escalate. It's amazing how much easier everything becomes when you catch it early."

Erica, meanwhile, had developed trust in Mr. Rivera's support and began using their agreed-upon signal—a simple hand gesture—when she felt overwhelmed. "He actually listens now," she told Ms. Jackson during a check-in. "He doesn't just think I'm being lazy."

Ripple Effects in the Classroom

The transformation extended beyond their individual relationship. Other students began to notice the different dynamic and felt safer expressing their own struggles. Maria, who had been quietly failing but afraid to ask for help, approached Mr. Rivera after seeing how he responded to Erica's difficulties.

"The whole classroom feels different," Ms. Jackson observed. "When students see that their teacher can handle big emotions and conflicts with understanding rather than punishment, they're more willing to take risks and be honest about their challenges."

Systemic Integration

Perhaps most importantly, Mr. Rivera began applying these principles with other students and sharing his insights with colleagues. During a professional development session, he reflected: "I used to think my job was to deliver content and manage behavior. Now I understand that my primary job is creating conditions where learning can happen—and that starts with helping students feel safe and understood."

The school administration took notice of the decreased behavioral referrals from Mr. Rivera's classroom and invited him to share his approach with other teachers. Ms. Jackson was asked to provide more training on neurobiological approaches to classroom management.

Long-term Student Outcomes

Erica's academic performance improved steadily, not just because of accommodations but because she was no longer expending emotional energy on defense and could direct her resources toward learning. Her relationship with Mr. Rivera became a template for how she approached other challenging relationships, both with adults and peers.

"She learned that conflict doesn't have to destroy relationships," Ms. Jackson noted. "In fact, working through difficulties can actually make relationships stronger. That's a life skill that will serve her far beyond middle school."

Measuring Transformation

The success of their approach could be measured in multiple ways:

Quantitative Changes:

- Zero behavioral referrals for Erica in the following semester
- Improved test scores and assignment completion
- Decreased absenteeism
- Other students in the class showing increased help-seeking behaviors

Qualitative Indicators:

- Stronger teacher-student relationships throughout the school
- Increased teacher confidence in handling challenging situations
- Students reporting feeling safer and more supported
- Parents noting positive changes in their children's attitudes toward school

Cultural Shifts:

- Teachers requesting more training in relationship-based approaches
- Administrative policies beginning to reflect trauma-informed principles

- Peer relationships improving as students learned conflict resolution skills
- Overall school climate surveys showing increased sense of belonging

This follow-up story illustrates a crucial principle: transformative crisis intervention isn't about perfect outcomes, but about creating new patterns of interaction that build resilience over time. When we respond to crisis moments with understanding rather than control, we don't just solve immediate problems—we teach new ways of being in relationship that can last a lifetime.

The neurobiological changes that occurred during their initial conflict resolution—the shift from defensive to connected states, the experience of feeling heard and understood, the empowerment through meaningful choice—created new neural pathways that supported ongoing growth and healing for everyone involved.

Transactional versus Transformative Crisis Intervention

The interactions between Erica, Mr. Rivera, and Ms. Jackson demonstrate a pivotal distinction in crisis response approaches. When Mr. Rivera initially confronted Erica, he employed what we recognize as a transactional approach. When Ms. Jackson intervened, she demonstrated a fundamentally different philosophy, a transformative approach.

The Transactional Approach

Traditional crisis management often relies on transactional interactions—exchanges focused on stopping unwanted behavior quickly, enforcing rules and maintaining order, implementing short-term solutions, maintaining power hierarchies where the authority figure directs the person in crisis, and achieving control as the primary goal.

When Mr. Rivera responded with "Sit down right now, young lady!" and "This behavior is completely unacceptable!" he was employing the traditional approach that prioritizes immediate compliance and consequences. While these methods may change visible behavior temporarily, they rarely address the underlying neurobiological state driving the behavior.

Transactional approaches often interpret challenging behavior as willful misconduct requiring discipline, counter escalation with authority and consequences, create threat cycles that intensify defensive responses, leave people feeling "managed" rather than understood, and strengthen defensive patterns over time as survival adaptations are met with control rather than understanding.

The Transformative Approach

Transformative interactions engage with the whole person and their dysregulated nervous system. These approaches recognize that challenging behavior communicates something meaningful about internal state, prioritize creating safety and supporting co-regulation before addressing behavior, offer regulated presence as a resource for nervous system stabilization, respond to defensive adaptations with understanding rather than control, and create lasting neurobiological change through repeated experiences of attunement.

Ms. Jackson's intervention demonstrated transformative principles through safety first by creating separate spaces for both individuals to regulate, choice and autonomy by asking "Would you like to take a short break with me?" neurobiological education by explaining "That happens to us when we feel threatened," regulated presence by maintaining calm, low voice and non-threatening posture, co-regulation by using her own nervous system stability to help others regulate, and repair and restoration by facilitating a conversation focused on understanding and prevention.

Core Principles of Transformative Crisis Intervention

Principle 1: De-escalation and Safety First

The highest priority in any crisis is establishing safety—not just physical safety, but neurobiological safety. This means reducing threat cues by lowering your voice rather than raising it, creating physical space rather than moving closer, softening facial expressions and body posture, and eliminating demands or ultimatums in the immediate moment.

Supporting autonomic regulation involves offering choices about environment, position, or activity, providing movement options when appropriate, creating calm, predictable interactions, and respecting the person's need for time and space.

Principle 2: Respect Autonomy During Dysregulation

When someone's nervous system is activated, their capacity for rational decision-making is compromised. However, this doesn't mean removing all choice. Instead, offer simple, clear options that respect agency, avoid forcing compliance when possible, recognize that resistance often signals a need for more safety, and allow people to maintain some control over their environment and responses.

When Erica declared "I'm not going back in there," Ms. Jackson respected this decision rather than forcing compliance. This respect for autonomy helped Erica feel safer and more willing to engage in the regulatory process.

Principle 3: Address All Activated Nervous Systems

Crisis situations rarely involve just one dysregulated person. In the classroom scenario, both Erica and Mr. Rivera were in defensive states, each triggering the other's nervous system. Effective intervention requires recognizing when multiple people are activated, avoiding taking sides or blaming, supporting regulation for all parties involved, and understanding how defensive states create reciprocal cycles.

Principle 4: Create Time and Space for Regulation

Regulation cannot be rushed. The nervous system needs time to shift from defensive states back to connection and calm. This means avoiding immediate problem-solving when someone is activated, allowing for cooling-off periods, recognizing that meaningful conversation requires regulated nervous systems, and planning restorative conversations after regulation has occurred.

Principle 5: Use Neurobiological Explanations

Framing crisis behavior through a neurobiological lens reduces shame and increases understanding. When Ms. Jackson explained, "When we feel threatened, our thinking brain goes offline and our survival brain takes over," she normalized the experience as human rather than pathological, reduced blame and judgment, created a framework for understanding future responses, and honored the adaptive nature of defensive reactions.

The Neural Science of Empathic Connection

At the heart of transformative crisis management lies the remarkable human capacity for empathy. While early research suggested mirror neurons provided the neurobiological foundation for empathy, recent meta-analyses indicate the relationship is more complex than initially thought. However, empathic connections clearly involve sophisticated neurobiological processes that can help shift nervous systems from states of defense to states of connection.

When we offer genuine empathy during crisis moments, we're engaging multiple neurobiological mechanisms. Autonomic nervous system synchronization allows our nervous systems to communicate continuously through subtle cues including facial expressions, vocal tone, breathing patterns, and body language. This creates opportunities for co-regulation where a regulated person can help guide a dysregulated person's nervous system toward greater balance.

Neurochemical benefits occur through positive empathic interactions that trigger the release of neurochemicals that counteract stress hormones and promote healing. Oxytocin reduces anxiety and increases trust, endorphins provide natural stress relief, dopamine creates motivation and facilitates learning, and serotonin supports emotional balance. These neurochemicals not only create immediate positive feelings but also support the growth of new neural connections, enhancing resilience over time (Siegel, 2012).

Practicing Empathy in Crisis Situations

The practice of empathy involves attuning to emotional states by noticing the subtle signs of nervous system activation—breathing patterns, muscle tension, facial expressions, vocal tone. Reflecting understanding through statements like "I can see you're really upset right now" or "That must have been overwhelming." Validating the legitimacy of feelings recognizes that all emotions are valid responses to perceived circumstances, even when the perception may be distorted by past experiences. Creating shared experiences finds moments of genuine connection that help the person feel less alone in their struggle.

Practical Strategies for Different Response Patterns

Supporting Fight Responses

When someone is in a fight state, they're biologically prepared for conflict. Effective strategies include environmental modifications such as creating more physical space, reducing stimulation (lighting, noise, visual clutter), removing audience when possible, and ensuring clear exit routes.

Communication approaches involve using calm, low vocal tones, speaking slowly and clearly, avoiding arguing or defending, and acknowledging their perspective without agreeing. Regulatory supports include offering movement opportunities (pacing, walking), providing time for the stress response to naturally decline, and using grounding techniques (feeling feet on floor, naming objects in room).

Supporting Flight Responses

Flight responses involve a biological need to create distance from perceived threat. Strategies include honoring the need for movement by providing safe spaces to move, offering walking breaks, allowing position changes, and respecting requests for distance.

Creating controlled escape options involves providing clear exit paths, permission to step away, scheduled check-ins rather than constant supervision, and gradual re-engagement as the nervous system settles.

Supporting Freeze Responses

When someone is in a freeze state, their nervous system has essentially gone offline. This requires patience and gentle presence by avoiding demands for immediate response, offering quiet, consistent presence, using soft, rhythmic sounds or movements, and providing comfort items (blankets, fidget tools).

Gradual re-engagement starts with simple, non-threatening activities, builds slowly toward more complex interactions, respects the time needed for nervous system reactivation, and celebrates small signs of engagement.

Supporting Flock Responses

When someone seeks safety through connection, provide appropriate social support by allowing proximity to trusted persons when possible, creating group activities that feel safe, respecting attachment needs without fostering unhealthy dependence, and building networks of support rather than single-person dependency.

Supporting Fawn Responses

Fawning involves people-pleasing as a survival strategy. Support includes creating safety for authentic expression by asking specifically for their preferences or opinions, validating their right to have different perspectives, avoiding praising compliance without checking for genuine consent, and modeling healthy boundary-setting.

Creating Environments that Support Regulation

The physical and social environment profoundly impacts nervous system regulation. Trauma-informed environments include physical environment factors such as natural lighting when possible, reduced noise levels, comfortable temperatures, pleasant, non-overwhelming scents, and soft textures and comfortable seating.

Safety and predictability involve clear sight lines and exit routes, consistent organization and layout, minimal visual clutter, posted schedules and expectations, and spaces for privacy and retreat.

Social environment factors include relational safety through consistent, trustworthy staff, clear, fair boundaries and expectations, respect for individual differences, opportunities for meaningful choice, and celebration of growth and effort.

Cultural responsiveness involves recognition of diverse communication styles, respect for cultural values and practices, inclusion of community and family wisdom, and awareness of historical and cultural trauma impacts.

Building Co-Regulatory Relationships

Co-regulation—the process by which a regulated nervous system helps bring another into regulation—forms the foundation of transformative crisis intervention.

Characteristics of Co-Regulatory Relationships

Consistency provides reliable presence and predictable responses that help the nervous system anticipate safety. Attunement involves the ability to accurately read and respond to another's emotional and physiological state. Differentiation means maintaining your own regulation while staying emotionally connected to someone in distress. Repair encompasses the capacity to acknowledge and address relationship ruptures when they occur. Appropriate boundaries create clear limits that create safety for both parties while maintaining connection.

Developing Co-Regulatory Skills

Self-awareness involves noticing your own nervous system responses and triggers. You cannot regulate someone else if you're dysregulated yourself. Somatic awareness means paying attention to breathing, muscle tension, heart rate, and other bodily sensations that signal your state. Emotional regulation develops strategies for maintaining your own balance during challenging interactions. Patience understands that nervous system change takes time and cannot be rushed. Cultural humility recognizes that safety and regulation may look different across cultures and individuals.

Common Challenges and Solutions in Implementation

Challenge: When Your Own Nervous System Gets Activated

One of the most common challenges in crisis intervention occurs when the responder's own nervous system becomes activated. This is normal and expected—our brains are designed to respond to threat cues, including those from other people's defensive states.

Signs of your own activation include increased heart rate or breathing, muscle tension, especially in jaw, shoulders, or hands, urge to raise your voice or move quickly, feeling defensive, frustrated, or overwhelmed, and loss of empathy or curiosity about the other person.

Strategies for self-regulation involve taking three deep breaths, focusing on lengthening the exhale, feeling your feet on the ground and noticing your physical presence, reminding yourself: "This person's behavior is about their nervous system, not about me," using positive self-talk: "I can stay calm and helpful," and taking a brief break if possible to restore your regulation.

Challenge: When Multiple People Are Activated

Crisis situations often involve multiple dysregulated individuals creating cycles of mutual activation. This requires a systems-level approach with assessment priorities to identify who is most activated and potentially unsafe, notice who might be available for co-regulation, and assess environmental factors that might be escalating the situation.

Intervention strategies include addressing safety first by separating highly activated individuals if needed, working with the most regulated person first to create a stabilizing influence, using the environment to support regulation (lighting, noise, space), and avoiding taking sides or assigning blame.

Challenge: Cultural Differences in Crisis Expression

Different cultures have varying norms around emotional expression, help-seeking, and authority relationships. What looks like resistance might be cultural communication patterns.

Cultural considerations involve learning about the cultural backgrounds of those you serve, understanding how trauma may be expressed differently across cultures, recognizing that eye contact, physical space, and vocal tone have cultural meanings, involving cultural liaisons or community elders when appropriate, and adapting your approach while maintaining core neurobiological principles.

Building Sustainable Crisis Response Systems

Effective crisis intervention requires more than individual skills—it requires systems that support both the people in crisis and those helping them.

Supporting Staff Regulation and Resilience

Crisis responders need ongoing support to maintain their own nervous system health through regular supervision that includes attention to the neurobiological impact of crisis work, opportunities to process difficult cases, and strategies for maintaining personal regulation.

Training in self-care goes beyond general wellness to include specific nervous system regulation practices like breathing techniques, mindfulness practices, and somatic awareness. Organizational policies acknowledge the neurobiological impact of crisis work, provide adequate rest between difficult cases, and create cultures of support rather than blame.

Creating Trauma Responsive Organizational Cultures

Organizations themselves can either support or hinder nervous system regulation. Physical environment factors include adequate lighting, comfortable temperatures, options for privacy, clear sight lines and exits, and spaces for movement and regulation.

Relational environment factors encompass consistent, trustworthy leadership, clear and fair policies, respect for individual differences, opportunities for meaningful input, and cultures that normalize rather than pathologize stress responses.

Policy considerations include trauma-informed disciplinary procedures, flexibility in how services are delivered, staff support during crisis situations, and regular assessment of organizational stress factors.

Conclusion

Transformative crisis intervention represents a fundamental shift from managing behavior to supporting nervous system regulation. By understanding that challenging behaviors emerge from sophisticated brain systems designed for survival, we can respond with approaches that create safety rather than increase threat.

The practical strategies outlined in this chapter, from co-regulation techniques to environmental modifications, all serve the same core purpose: helping dysregulated nervous systems return to states where connection, learning, and growth become possible.

This work requires not only understanding neurobiological principles but also developing the personal and professional capacities to remain regulated in the face of others' distress. When we can offer our own regulated presence as a resource, we create opportunities for genuine transformation rather than mere compliance.

The case of Erica and Mr. Rivera demonstrates how quickly crisis situations can shift when met with understanding rather than control. By recognizing that both student and teacher were caught in protective states, Ms. Jackson created pathways back to connection and learning. This is the essence of transformative crisis intervention: meeting defensive adaptations with curiosity and care, trusting in the nervous system's capacity for regulation and healing.

The principles explored here extend far beyond crisis situations into all our relationships and interactions. When we understand that all human behavior emerges from the dance between safety and threat detection, connection and protection, we can approach each other with greater compassion and more effective support.

Questions for Personal Reflection or Group Discussion

Consider these questions individually or discuss with colleagues to deepen your understanding of how to move from reactive crisis management to transformative approaches.

Understanding Your Approach

1. **Identifying Your Default Style** Reflect on a recent crisis situation you handled. Did you approach it more transactionally (focused on stopping behavior quickly) or transformatively (focused on understanding and connection)? What factors influenced your approach?

2. **Recognizing Co-Regulation Opportunities** Think about your own nervous system regulation during challenging interactions. How does your internal state affect others around you? What helps you maintain a regulated presence when others are dysregulated?

Application to Your Practice

3. **Environmental Assessment** Evaluate your current work environment through the lens of nervous system regulation. What physical and social elements support regulation? What factors might inadvertently trigger defensive responses?
4. **Cultural Considerations** Consider the diverse populations you serve. How might cultural differences in crisis expression or help-seeking behavior require adaptations to your approach while maintaining core principles of dignity and respect?

Systemic Reflection

5. **Organizational Support** How does your organization currently support both the people in crisis and those helping them? What changes would better support sustainable, transformative crisis response?

Integration Practice: Over the next week, before entering any potentially challenging interaction, take three breaths and set an intention to prioritize connection over control. Notice how this shifts both your approach and the outcomes.

References

Perry, B. D. (2009). Examining child maltreatment through a neurodevelopmental lens: Clinical applications of the neurosequential model of therapeutics. Journal of Loss and Trauma, 14(4), 240-255.

Porges, S. W. (2011). The polyvagal theory: Neurophysiological foundations of emotions, attachment, communication, and self-regulation. W. W. Norton & Company.

Schore, A. N. (2003). Affect dysregulation and disorders of the self. W. W. Norton & Company.

Siegel, D. J. (2012). The developing mind: How relationships and the brain interact to shape who we are (2nd ed.). Guilford Press.

Chapter 3: Developmental Trauma and Healing Through Relationship

While understanding crisis response in the moment is crucial, lasting transformation requires us to examine how early experiences shape the very architecture of response patterns. This chapter explores how developmental trauma affects the nervous system and, more importantly, how healing relationships can literally rewire neural pathways throughout the lifespan.

Understanding crisis response requires examining not just what happens in the moment of dysregulation, but how early experiences shape the very architecture of the nervous system. This chapter explores the profound impact of developmental trauma on brain development and demonstrates how healing relationships can literally rewire neural pathways throughout the lifespan.

We'll examine how the brain develops in relationship, how early adverse experiences alter this development, and most importantly, how therapeutic relationships and supportive environments can harness the brain's remarkable capacity for change. This understanding transforms crisis intervention from behavior management to neurobiological healing.

The Developing Brain: From Bottom to Top

To fully understand crisis behavior, we must appreciate how brain development unfolds and how early experiences, particularly traumatic ones, shape this development. Research in developmental neuroscience shows that the human brain develops in a sequential, hierarchical manner, from the bottom up (Perry, 2009).

The brainstem develops first, regulating our most basic functions including breathing, heart rate, and body temperature. The diencephalon, including the hypothalamus, develops next, coordinating sleep, hunger, and basic drives. The limbic system follows, governing emotional responses and attachment. The cortex develops last, with the prefrontal regions continuing to mature into early adulthood.

This sequential development has profound implications for understanding behavior during crisis. When threatened, higher-order thinking systems become less accessible while more primitive survival systems take control. A person in crisis may literally not have access to their rational thinking capacities—not by choice, but by neurobiological design.

The Right Brain: Foundation of Emotional Development

Allan Schore's groundbreaking research has illuminated the critical role of the right hemisphere in attachment and emotional development. Unlike the left hemisphere, which develops later and specializes in language and logic, the right brain matures earlier and processes emotional and social information. This hemisphere is dominant during our first three years of life—a period Schore calls the "critical period of emotional development" (Schore, 2003).

The right brain is responsible for processing nonverbal emotional communication, regulating stress responses and emotional states, maintaining our sense of self and bodily awareness, enabling empathy and social connection, and storing implicit memories of relational experiences.

Understanding right-brain dominance in early development helps explain why traditional verbal interventions often fail during crisis moments. When someone is dysregulated, they've shifted into right-brain processing modes that don't respond well to left-brain logical explanations.

Neuroplasticity: The Brain's Capacity for Change

The brain's remarkable adaptability, known as neuroplasticity, is both a vulnerability and an opportunity. During early development, the brain is exceptionally plastic—forming neural connections at an astonishing rate based on environmental input. This plasticity makes young children particularly vulnerable to adverse experiences, but it also creates tremendous potential for healing through supportive relationships and environments.

Key principles of neuroplasticity include experience-dependent development, where the brain literally develops based on the experiences it receives. Repeated experiences create stronger neural pathways, while unused connections are pruned away. Critical periods offer certain developmental windows with enhanced plasticity. Early intervention during these periods tends to be more effective than later intervention.

Sequential development means the brain organizes from bottom to top, so foundational systems must be stable before higher-order functions can develop optimally. Lifelong capacity exists because while early developmental windows offer the greatest plasticity, the brain maintains capacity for change across the lifespan through meaningful experiences and relationships (Siegel, 2012).

Understanding Early Childhood Trauma and Its Impact

Early childhood trauma fundamentally alters developmental trajectories, particularly in systems involved in stress response, emotional regulation, and social engagement. These alterations are not character flaws or choices, but adaptations to environments where danger was real and resources for protection were limited.

The Adaptive Nature of Trauma Responses

What we often label as "maladaptive behaviors" typically began as creative survival strategies. Through the lens of neurobiology, we can recognize that challenging behaviors often represent adaptations that protected against overwhelming threat, managed unbearable emotional states, secured whatever attachment was available, and made sense in the original traumatic context.

As van der Kolk (2014) emphasizes, trauma fundamentally changes how the mind and brain manage perceptions, affecting not only how we think but our very capacity to think. Trauma survivors often continue to organize their lives as if the trauma were still occurring, with their energy focused on suppressing inner chaos rather than engaging spontaneously with life.

For example, hypervigilance—scanning constantly for danger—is an extraordinarily effective survival strategy in dangerous environments. Emotional numbing protects against overwhelming feelings when escape isn't possible. These adaptations can become problematic when they persist in safer environments, but they deserve respect as survival resources that served essential purposes.

The Polyvagal Perspective on Developmental Trauma

Through the lens of Polyvagal Theory, we can understand developmental trauma as creating lasting patterns in how the nervous system responds to perceived safety and threat. Early experiences that violate expectations, such as abuse from caregivers, can lead to chronic defensive reaction patterns where the ability to recognize safety is disrupted and even safe environments trigger defensive responses.

Children who experience consistent danger or unpredictable caregiving develop nervous systems that activate defensive circuits (mobilization or immobilization) more readily, have greater difficulty returning to regulated states, struggle to recognize and respond to safety cues, may interpret neutral stimuli as threatening, and have fewer experiences of the social engagement state where learning and connection flourish.

These patterns manifest in behavioral responses that can be misinterpreted as oppositional, unmotivated, or deliberately troublemaking. In reality, they represent a nervous system organized around survival rather than connection or exploration.

The Neurobiology of Developmental Trauma

Developmental trauma affects multiple brain systems simultaneously. Stress response systems become hyperactive, with elevated baseline cortisol levels and exaggerated responses to minor stressors. The HPA (hypothalamic-pituitary-adrenal) axis becomes dysregulated, creating patterns of chronic stress activation.

Memory systems are impacted, with traumatic experiences stored as fragmented sensory and emotional memories rather than coherent narratives. This leads to trauma responses being triggered by sensory cues that remind the nervous system of past danger.

Attachment systems are disrupted when caregivers are sources of both safety and threat. This creates disorganized attachment patterns where the child simultaneously seeks and fears closeness.

Self-regulation capacities fail to develop optimally when caregivers cannot provide consistent co-regulation. The child's nervous system doesn't learn to return to calm states effectively.

The Power of Relationship in Neurobiological Healing

Perhaps the most crucial finding from trauma neuroscience is that healing happens in relationship. The same neurobiological systems that are damaged by relational trauma can be restored through consistent, attuned relationships. For children spending six to eight hours daily in educational settings, teachers and support staff become critical agents of this healing process.

The Centrality of Co-Regulation

Co-regulation provides the foundation for developing self-regulatory capacity. Through thousands of co-regulatory experiences, children (and adults) gradually develop neural networks that support independent regulation.

As Schore (2003) emphasizes, self-regulation is preceded by co-regulation. The capacity to regulate emotional states develops within the context of caregiving relationships where the caregiver helps modulate the child's arousal by attuning to their internal state and responding appropriately. Over time, through repeated co-regulatory interactions, the child develops the neural architecture to regulate their own states.

For those with developmental trauma, these co-regulatory experiences may have been missing, inconsistent, or themselves sources of threat.

Therapeutic relationships and supportive environments can provide the missing co-regulatory experiences that build new neural pathways.

Neurobiological Mechanisms of Relationship-Based Healing

Several key neurobiological mechanisms explain why relationships are so powerful in healing trauma. Autonomic nervous system attunement occurs because our autonomic nervous systems communicate continuously with those around us through subtle cues including facial expressions, vocal tone, breathing patterns, and body language. This nonverbal communication happens below conscious awareness but profoundly influences our sense of safety. In supportive relationships, this autonomic attunement allows a regulated person to gradually guide a dysregulated person's nervous system toward greater balance.

Neurochemical benefits emerge from positive social interactions that trigger the release of neurochemicals that counteract stress hormones and promote healing. These neurochemicals not only create immediate positive feelings but also support the growth of new neural connections, enhancing resilience over time.

Right-brain to right-brain communication, as demonstrated by Schore's research, shows that healing happens through right-brain to right-brain communication between caregiver and child, or therapist and client. This involves nonverbal attunement to emotional states and the sharing of regulatory capacity through the relationship itself.

The Healing Role of Educational and Treatment Settings

Educators and treatment providers often represent the first stable, predictable relationships that traumatized children encounter outside their families. Their daily interactions—from morning greetings to responses during challenging moments—have the potential to literally rewire developing brains.

Characteristics of healing relationships share several key qualities. Consistency provides reliable presence and predictable responses that help the nervous system anticipate safety rather than threat. Attunement involves the ability to accurately read and respond to another's emotional and physiological state without becoming overwhelmed by it.

Differentiation means maintaining one's own regulation while staying emotionally connected to someone in distress. This allows the regulated person to serve as an external regulator for the dysregulated person. Repair encompasses the capacity to acknowledge and address relationship ruptures when they occur. This teaches that relationships can survive conflict and that repair is possible.

Appropriate boundaries create clear limits that create safety for both parties while maintaining connection and care.

Creating Co-Regulatory Environments

Physical and social environments can either support or hinder co-regulation. Physical environment factors include natural lighting when possible, reduced noise levels and sensory overwhelm, comfortable temperatures and seating options, clear sight lines and exit routes for safety, spaces for privacy and retreat when needed, and natural elements like plants or water sounds.

Social environment factors encompass consistent, trustworthy staff and clear expectations, cultures that value emotional awareness and regulation, multiple opportunities for positive social connection, recognition of individual differences in regulatory needs, and celebration of growth and effort rather than just outcomes.

Cultural and Historical Trauma: Expanding Our Understanding

Our understanding of trauma must extend beyond individual experiences to include cultural and historical dimensions. Many communities have experienced collective trauma through colonization, genocide, forced migration, enslavement, and systematic oppression. These experiences create intergenerational patterns that influence how individuals perceive and respond to threat.

Historical Trauma and Its Transmission

Historical trauma has been defined as cumulative emotional and psychological wounding over the lifespan and across generations, emanating from massive group trauma experiences. The historical trauma response includes depression, self-destructive behavior, suicidal thoughts and gestures, anxiety, low self-esteem, anger, and difficulty recognizing and expressing emotions.

Research suggests that trauma can be transmitted across generations through multiple pathways including epigenetic changes that alter gene expression, disrupted attachment patterns passed from parent to child, cultural narratives and family stories about danger and survival, and ongoing exposure to discrimination and oppression.

Cultural humility becomes particularly crucial when working with communities that have experienced historical trauma, as it requires practitioners to recognize the systemic racism and intergenerational trauma that continues to affect marginalized groups. Rather than making assumptions about cultural experiences, culturally humble crisis responders center and empower individuals on their healing journey, avoiding authoritative, power-over communication styles that may replicate historical patterns of oppression (Ranjbar et al., 2020).

Cultural Humility in Crisis Response

Effective crisis responders develop cultural humility—a concept originally developed by physicians Melanie Tervalon and Jann Murray-Garcia (1998) as a lifelong commitment to self-evaluation and self-critique, to redressing power imbalances, and to developing mutually beneficial partnerships with communities—adapted here as the capacity to recognize the limitations of their own cultural perspective and learn from the lived experiences of those they serve. This approach involves acknowledging cultural differences in how safety and threat are perceived, recognizing culture-specific manifestations of defensive responses, understanding cultural variations in regulation practices and healing traditions, respecting cultural strengths and resources for healing, and learning from community wisdom about effective support.

Recent research emphasizes that trauma-responsive care can be enhanced by adopting an attitude of cultural humility because traumatic events are always embedded in a cultural context and identity (Ranjbar et al., 2020). Foronda and colleagues' (2016) concept analysis identified that cultural humility involves five key attributes: openness, self-awareness, egoless interactions, supportive interactions, and self-reflection and critique, all of which align with the neurobiological principles of creating safety and supporting regulation discussed throughout this chapter.

Research in psychology demonstrates that when helpers approach their work with cultural humility—characterized by respect and lack of superiority toward cultural backgrounds—stronger therapeutic alliances develop, leading to better outcomes (Hook et al., 2013). This finding aligns with neurobiological principles: when individuals feel culturally seen and respected, their nervous systems are more likely to move toward states of safety and openness, creating optimal conditions for healing and growth.

By integrating cultural awareness with neurobiological understanding, we create more inclusive and effective crisis response systems.

Practical Applications: Creating Healing Communities

Beyond the Dyad: Systems-Level Healing

The same principles that guide individual crisis intervention—what we'll later explore as the MindSet Four-Step Model of Acknowledgment, Acceptance, Validation, and Empowerment—apply to creating healing communities. When we understand that challenging behaviors communicate unmet needs rather than represent moral failings, we can respond with approaches that support nervous system regulation while maintaining appropriate boundaries.

While one-to-one relationships are powerful, truly transformative healing often requires a broader community of support. The nervous system evolved to function within a social network, not just in isolated relationships.

Effective healing communities provide multiple opportunities for co-regulatory experiences across different relationships, cultures that normalize developmental variation in regulatory capacity, shared responsibility for supporting regulation rather than placing all burden on individual relationships, recognition of systemic factors that contribute to dysregulation, and advocacy for policy changes that support neurobiological healing.

Trauma-Responsive Organizational Practices

Organizations committed to neurobiological healing implement practices that support nervous system regulation at every level. Leadership approaches model regulation, create psychological safety, provide consistent and predictable structures, and acknowledge the neurobiological impact of their work on staff.

Policy development includes trauma-responsive disciplinary procedures, flexibility in service delivery, support for staff during crisis situations, and regular assessment of organizational stress factors.

Training and supervision encompasses education about neurobiological impacts of trauma, skill development in co-regulation, opportunities to process difficult cases, and support for staff's own healing journeys.

Environmental design considers sensory factors, provides options for regulation and retreat, creates clear and predictable physical layouts, and incorporates elements that support nervous system calm.

Ethical Dimensions of Trauma-Responsive Practice

Working with neurobiological healing principles raises several ethical considerations.

The Ethics of Power and Relationship

Understanding nervous system vulnerability requires careful attention to how power is used in helping relationships. This includes recognizing that dysregulated nervous systems are more susceptible to influence, using knowledge of neurobiology to support rather than manipulate, maintaining appropriate boundaries while providing co-regulatory support, and acknowledging when our own trauma histories may impact our responses.

The Ethics of Hope and Realistic Expectations

Neuroplasticity research offers tremendous hope for healing, but it's important to maintain realistic expectations. Change takes time and often involves setbacks. Not all trauma impacts can be completely resolved. Individual differences affect recovery trajectories. Systemic factors continue to impact individual healing.

The Ethics of Narrative and Meaning-Making

How we explain behavior and trauma impacts both intervention approaches and self-understanding. This involves moving from pathologizing narratives to adaptive ones, honoring survival strategies while supporting growth, creating space for individuals to author their own healing stories, and avoiding oversimplification of complex trauma impacts.

Supporting Resilience Across the Lifespan

While this chapter has focused primarily on early development, the principles of neurobiological healing apply across the lifespan. Adults who experienced early trauma can still benefit from co-regulatory relationships and neurobiologically-informed support.

Adult Neuroplasticity and Healing

Research demonstrates that adult brains maintain significant capacity for change. New neural pathways can develop through meaningful relationships. Mindfulness and somatic practices can support nervous system regulation. Therapeutic relationships can provide corrective emotional experiences. Community connections can offer ongoing co-regulatory support.

Supporting Healing in Families and Communities

Individual healing often requires support for entire family and community systems. This includes parent education that includes neurobiological understanding, community programs that provide co-regulatory experiences, policy advocacy that addresses systemic sources of trauma, and cultural healing practices that honor community wisdom and traditions.

Conclusion

Understanding developmental trauma through a neurobiological lens transforms our approach to crisis intervention and healing. Rather than seeing challenging behaviors as moral failings or conscious choices, we can recognize them as sophisticated adaptations that helped individuals survive overwhelming experiences.

This perspective opens pathways for profound healing through relationship. When we understand that the same neural systems damaged by relational trauma can be restored through attuned connections, we recognize the tremendous responsibility and opportunity inherent in every interaction with someone who has experienced trauma.

The brain's capacity for neuroplasticity means that healing is possible throughout the lifespan, though it requires patience, consistency, and deep respect for the survival wisdom embedded in defensive adaptations. By creating environments and relationships that support nervous system regulation, we can help individuals develop new neural pathways that support not just survival, but genuine thriving.

Ultimately, this work requires us to examine not just individual trauma histories, but the systemic and cultural factors that contribute to trauma and healing. True transformation occurs when we address trauma at multiple levels—individual, relational, community, and societal—recognizing that healing happens in connection and community.

The journey from trauma to healing is not about returning to some previous state, but about growing new capacities for regulation, connection, and meaning-making. When we approach this work with neurobiological understanding, cultural humility, and deep respect for human resilience, we create conditions where profound transformation becomes possible.

Cycle of Neurobiological Healing

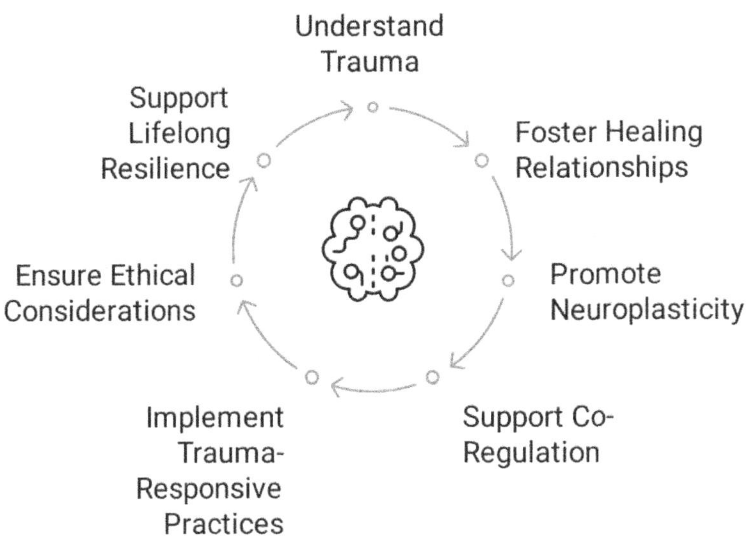

Questions for Personal Reflection or Group Discussion

Consider these questions individually or discuss with colleagues to deepen your understanding of how early experiences shape response patterns and how healing happens through relationship.

Understanding Development and Trauma

1. **Reframing "Challenging" Behaviors** Think of someone whose behavior you find difficult to understand. How might viewing their responses as creative survival strategies rather than character flaws change your approach? What adaptive purpose might their behavior have served?
2. **Your Own Developmental Awareness** Reflect on your own early experiences with safety, connection, and stress. How do these experiences influence your responses to others in crisis? What triggers or patterns do you notice in yourself?

Application to Your Practice

3. **Creating Co-Regulatory Experiences** Consider your daily interactions with those you serve. In what ways do you currently provide co-regulatory support? How could you intentionally create more opportunities for healing through consistent, attuned relationship?

4. **Cultural and Historical Trauma Awareness** How might historical and cultural trauma impact the communities you serve? What steps can you take to approach your work with greater cultural humility while maintaining neurobiologically-informed principles?

Systemic Reflection

5. **Organizational Healing Capacity** Evaluate your organization's capacity to provide healing relationships. What policies, practices, or structures support relationship-based healing? What changes would better support trauma-responsive care?

Integration Practice: This week, intentionally notice one person's behavior through the lens of nervous system adaptation rather than choice or defiance. Practice offering your regulated presence as a co-regulatory resource.

References

Janak, P. H., & Tye, K. M. (2015). From circuits to behaviour in the amygdala. *Nature*, 517(7534), 284-292.

LeDoux, J. E., & Pine, D. S. (2016). Using neuroscience to help understand fear and anxiety: A two-system framework. *American Journal of Psychiatry*, 173(11), 1083-1093.

Perry, B. D. (2009). Examining child maltreatment through a neurodevelopmental lens: Clinical applications of the neurosequential model of therapeutics. *Journal of Loss and Trauma*, 14(4), 240-255.

Porges, S. W. (2011). *The polyvagal theory: Neurophysiological foundations of emotions, attachment, communication, and self-regulation*. W. W. Norton & Company.

Schore, A. N. (2003). *Affect dysregulation and disorders of the self*. W. W. Norton & Company.

Tervalon, M., & Murray-Garcia, J. (1998). Cultural humility versus cultural competence: A critical distinction in defining physician training outcomes in multicultural education. *Journal of Health Care for the Poor and Underserved*, *9*(2), 117-125.

Chapter 4: The Science of Empathy in Crisis Response

Empathy is more than just a nice idea—it's a powerful neurobiological intervention that can shift crisis situations from escalation to resolution. This chapter examines the scientific foundations of empathic connection and demonstrates why understanding others' experiences proves so effective in navigating the most challenging moments.

Empathy is the cornerstone of transformative crisis management. But empathy is more than just feeling sorry for someone or agreeing with their perspective; it is the active, intentional practice of stepping into another's shoes, opening our hearts to their experiences—their pain, their hopes, and dreams—even when they differ from our own (Brown, 2018).

By cultivating this deep understanding, we pave the way for more profound connection and more effective crisis resolution. This chapter explores the scientific foundations of empathy in crisis situations, examining why empathic approaches prove so powerful in navigating interpersonal and organizational challenges during times of crisis.

The Neurobiological Foundation of Empathic Connection

Understanding why empathy works so effectively in crisis situations requires examining what happens in the brain during empathic exchanges. When individuals or organizations face crises, the brain's threat-detection system—primarily the amygdala—becomes highly activated, triggering fight-flight-freeze responses that narrow thinking and limit access to the prefrontal cortex, where complex problem-solving occurs (LeDoux & Pine, 2016).

This neurobiological reality explains why crisis situations so often lead to polarized thinking, reactive responses, and diminished creativity—precisely when these higher-order capacities are most needed. The brain's threat response, while adaptive for immediate physical dangers, proves maladaptive for navigating complex social and organizational challenges.

How Empathy Shifts Neurobiological States

Empathic engagement helps shift this neurobiological state in several documented ways. Feeling understood and supported reduces cortisol (stress hormone) levels while increasing oxytocin (the "connection" hormone), creating a neurochemical environment more conducive to collaboration and innovation (Taylor et al., 2000).

According to Polyvagal Theory, empathic exchanges can help activate the social engagement system, the neurobiological state most conducive to learning, connection, and creative problem-solving (Porges, 2011). By reducing threat responses, empathy helps restore access to the prefrontal cortex, expanding cognitive flexibility and enabling more creative crisis solutions (Siegel, 2012).

These neurobiological shifts explain why empathic approaches often succeed where purely rational or authoritative approaches fail during crises. When people feel threatened or dismissed, their neurobiological state makes productive engagement nearly impossible. By contrast, when they experience empathy, their brains literally function differently—accessing capacities for nuanced thinking, perspective-taking, and creative problem-solving that remain inaccessible in threat states.

The Psychology of Safety in Crisis Situations

Empathy has the remarkable ability to disarm defensiveness and create a sense of psychological safety (Edmondson, 1998). When an individual feels truly seen, heard, and understood, their defenses naturally begin to lower, enabling them to engage in dialogue with a more open heart and a clearer mind. This is crucial in crisis management, as it helps to prevent the escalation of tensions and fosters an environment conducive to finding common ground.

Psychological Safety as Crisis Infrastructure

The concept of psychological safety takes on particular significance during crises, when stakes are high and uncertainty abounds. Team members often possess critical information about emerging problems, potential solutions, or stakeholder concerns—yet may hesitate to share this information if they fear blame, dismissal, or retribution.

When psychological safety is present during crisis situations, individuals access higher-order thinking capabilities, engage in more creative problem-solving, demonstrate greater resilience under pressure, share information more readily, and collaborate more effectively across hierarchical levels. By contrast, when psychological safety is absent, team members' cognitive and emotional resources become consumed by self-protection, dramatically reducing their capacity to contribute to crisis resolution (Edmondson, 2019).

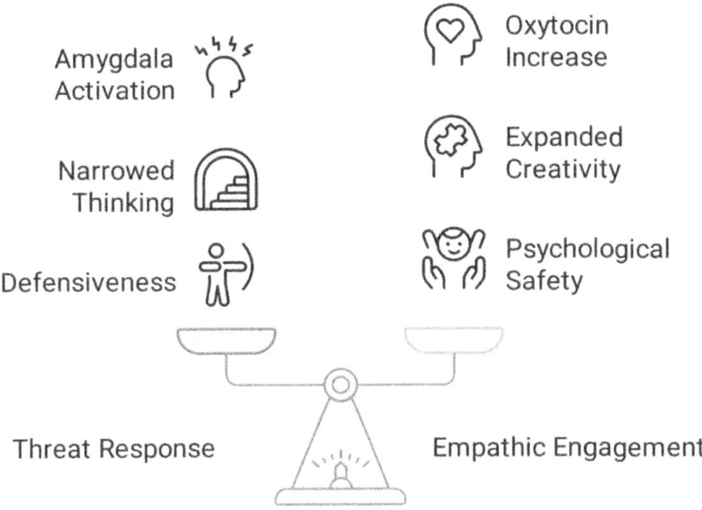

Validation Without Agreement

It's important to understand that one need not agree with another person's perspective on an issue to validate their feelings, beliefs, and behaviors. Research in educational and therapeutic settings demonstrates that when leaders prioritize validation before implementing consequences or solutions, individuals report experiencing greater emotional safety and an increased willingness to engage in problem-solving dialogue (van der Kolk, 2014).

When we take the time to acknowledge another person's perspective—even if we disagree with it—we send a powerful message that we value their viewpoint, that their experiences and opinions matter. This sense of validation can go a long way in calming emotions and building trust, laying the foundation for productive dialogue and potential resolution.

Empathy as Strategic Advantage in Crisis Management

Beyond the interpersonal realm, empathy serves as a strategic advantage in organizational and community crisis management. When leaders approach crises with an empathic mindset, they unlock several powerful advantages that traditional, purely tactical approaches cannot match.

Traditional crisis management often emphasizes message control, legal protection, and operational continuity—all important considerations, but insufficient on their own to address the human dimensions of crisis. Without empathy as a foundation, even the most technically sound crisis responses often fail to restore trust, heal relationships, or prevent recurring problems.

The Dual Dimensions of Crisis Empathy

In crisis management, empathy operates along two crucial dimensions: the internal dimension (within the organization or team) and the external dimension (with affected stakeholders, communities, or customers). Both dimensions require distinct yet complementary empathic approaches. This dual focus challenges the common tendency to prioritize either internal or external stakeholders during crises.

Organizations facing public criticism often focus exclusively on external messaging while neglecting the emotional impact on their own team members. Conversely, organizations experiencing internal turmoil may concentrate on employee needs while failing to consider how their challenges affect external stakeholders. Truly empathic crisis management addresses both dimensions simultaneously, recognizing their interdependence.

Internal Empathy: Creating Safety During Turbulence

During a crisis, team members often experience heightened stress, uncertainty, and fear. Leaders who prioritize empathy create what Edmondson (2019) terms "psychological safety"—an environment where team members feel secure enough to voice concerns, share information, and take necessary risks without fear of humiliation or punishment.

Traditional crisis leadership often emphasizes decisive action, clear authority, and simplified messaging—an approach that can inadvertently silence important voices, overlook critical information, and create the illusion of control in situations characterized by genuine uncertainty.

By contrast, empathic crisis leadership acknowledges complexity and uncertainty, invites multiple perspectives, and recognizes that the best solutions often emerge through collaborative sense-making rather than top-down directives. This approach requires leaders to embrace particular vulnerabilities, including acknowledging the limits of their knowledge, sharing authentic emotional responses (while maintaining appropriate boundaries), and relinquishing some control over both process and outcomes.

These vulnerabilities, while uncomfortable, create the conditions for authentic engagement that purely authoritative approaches cannot achieve.

External Empathy: The Foundation of Stakeholder Trust

The external dimension of crisis empathy focuses on understanding and addressing the needs, fears, and experiences of those affected by the crisis—customers, community members, shareholders, or the public. External empathy plays a particularly crucial role during crises that affect diverse stakeholder groups, each with distinct concerns, values, and perspectives.

Rather than approaching stakeholders as homogeneous audiences for crisis messaging, empathic leaders recognize the unique experiences and needs of different groups, tailoring both their understanding and their responses accordingly. By understanding and addressing stakeholders' core concerns—which often center on safety, respect, and feeling heard—organizations reduce the anger and alienation that fuel lawsuits, boycotts, and ongoing reputation damage.

The Attachment Science Behind Crisis Connection

Research in attachment theory provides crucial insights into why empathic approaches prove so effective during crisis situations. Attachment theory, originally developed by John Bowlby and significantly expanded through the neurobiological research of Allan Schore, demonstrates that humans have fundamental needs for safety, connection, and co-regulation that become heightened during times of stress (Schore, 2003).

Co-Regulation in Crisis Contexts

Co-regulation becomes particularly important during crisis situations. When individuals experience crisis-related stress, their capacity for self-regulation often becomes compromised. In these moments, the presence of a regulated, empathic other can provide external regulatory support that helps restore internal balance.

This process occurs through multiple channels. Nonverbal attunement involves matching breathing patterns, vocal tone, and body language. Emotional validation acknowledges and normalizes stress responses. Cognitive support helps organize overwhelming information and experiences. Relational presence provides consistent, reliable connection amid uncertainty.

Trauma-Responsive Understanding

Many individuals entering crisis situations carry histories of previous trauma that influence their responses to current stressors. Trauma-informed approaches recognize that behaviors which may appear resistant, oppositional, or irrational often represent adaptive responses to past experiences of threat or harm (van der Kolk, 2014).

This understanding shifts the fundamental question from "What's wrong with this person?" to "What has happened to this person, and how are they trying to stay safe?" This reframe opens possibilities for empathic connection that judgmental approaches foreclose.

From Understanding to Practice: The Power of "Yeah"

Having explored how empathy creates the neurobiological foundation for effective crisis resolution, we can identify a transformative indicator of success: the concept of "Evoking the Yeah." This represents the practical bridge between understanding the science of human connection and creating meaningful change in crisis situations.

The "yeah" response most often occurs during what we'll explore as the Validation step of the MindSet Four-Step Model—that moment when someone feels their experience has been truly understood and honored, even without agreement. The "yeah" response signifies that pivotal moment when someone feels truly seen and understood—when their nervous system shifts from a state of defense to one of connection. This isn't merely a superficial acknowledgment but rather a profound biological marker indicating that we've successfully created the conditions for genuine engagement and transformation.

Recognizing the "Yeah" Moment

This concept provides crisis leaders with a concrete, observable indicator of empathic connection. Rather than wondering whether their attempts at empathy are effective, leaders can watch for the "yeah" response—that moment when stakeholders' body language, tone, and engagement visibly shift from defensive to receptive.

Observable signs of the "yeah" response include physical relaxation, with shoulders dropping, breathing deepening, and facial tension releasing. Vocal changes become apparent as tone becomes less defensive, pace slows, and volume moderates. Cognitive shifts show as movement from position-defending to problem-exploring occurs. Relational opening manifests through increased eye contact, forward-leaning posture, and collaborative language.

This response signals that the neurobiological shift described earlier has occurred, creating the foundation for productive dialogue.

Barriers to Empathic Crisis Management

Despite its proven effectiveness, empathic crisis management faces several common barriers that limit its implementation. Understanding these barriers helps leaders proactively address them, creating conditions more conducive to empathic approaches, even amid pressure and complexity.

Time Pressure and the Urgency Bias

Perhaps the most pervasive barrier to empathic crisis management is the belief that empathy takes too much time. Amid urgent threats, organizations may feel they cannot "afford" to invest in understanding stakeholder experiences or building relational foundations for collaboration. This urgency bias leads many leaders to default to directive, control-oriented approaches that appear more efficient in the moment but often create longer-term complications.

Overcoming the urgency bias requires recognizing that empathy is an investment rather than merely a cost—that time devoted to understanding stakeholder experiences pays dividends through more effective solutions, stronger relationships, and reduced resistance. Research consistently demonstrates that time spent in empathic understanding actually accelerates overall crisis resolution by preventing the escalation cycles that consume far more time and resources (Siegel, 2012).

Empathy as "Weakness" Misconception

Another common barrier involves cultural associations between empathy and weakness—the assumption that understanding others' experiences somehow diminishes authority or signals capitulation to their demands. This misconception is particularly pronounced in organizational cultures that value toughness, decisiveness, and emotional detachment as leadership virtues.

Neuroscience research challenges this misconception by demonstrating that empathy actually requires significant cognitive and emotional sophistication. The capacity to understand multiple perspectives simultaneously, regulate one's own emotional responses while attending to others', and maintain clear thinking amid emotional intensity represents advanced rather than diminished leadership capability.

Fear of Emotional Contagion

Many leaders hesitate to engage empathically during crises due to fear of emotional contagion—concern that opening space for emotions might unleash overwhelming feelings that derail productive action. This fear often leads to attempts to "manage" emotions through minimization, rationalization, or diversion—approaches that typically intensify rather than resolve emotional distress.

Neuroscience research offers important insights into addressing this barrier. Studies show that acknowledging emotions actually reduces their intensity and duration, while suppression prolongs and intensifies emotional responses (van der Kolk, 2014). Moreover, emotions themselves provide crucial information during crises—signals about what matters to stakeholders, what they fear losing, and what they need to move forward constructively.

Cultural and Professional Conditioning

Professional training in many fields emphasizes analytical, objective approaches that may seem incompatible with empathic engagement. Medical, legal, engineering, and business education often prioritize technical expertise while providing little training in emotional intelligence or relational skills.

This conditioning can create internal conflict for crisis leaders who recognize the value of empathy but lack confidence in their ability to integrate it with their technical expertise. Overcoming this barrier requires reframing empathy not as abandoning professional competence but as enhancing it—recognizing that technical solutions implemented without empathic understanding often fail to achieve their intended outcomes.

Balancing Empathy with Boundaries

Effective crisis management requires transcending the false dichotomy between empathy and boundaries—recognizing that these elements complement rather than contradict each other. Leaders sometimes hesitate to employ empathic approaches due to concerns that understanding others' perspectives might require abandoning important boundaries or compromising core values.

The Integration of Care and Limits

In reality, the most effective crisis leaders integrate empathy and boundaries seamlessly, using clear limits to create psychological safety while employing empathic understanding to make those boundaries meaningful and constructive. This integration creates what family systems theorists term "loving confrontation"—engagement that combines genuine care with clear expectations.

The most effective boundaries in crisis situations share several characteristics. They demonstrate clarity, with expectations explicitly stated rather than merely implied. They serve clear purposes, with boundaries serving relationship goals rather than asserting power. They show flexibility, with limits adapting to changing circumstances while maintaining core principles. They embody mutuality, with expectations applying to all parties, including leaders themselves. They express compassion, with boundaries implemented with empathy for their impact.

When these qualities characterize crisis boundaries, they strengthen rather than diminish empathic connection—creating the psychological safety necessary for authentic engagement while preventing dynamics that would undermine genuine understanding.

Cultural Considerations in Crisis Empathy

Empathic crisis management must account for cultural differences in emotional expression, authority relationships, and help-seeking behaviors. What constitutes empathic response varies significantly across cultural contexts, requiring leaders to develop cultural humility alongside empathic capacity.

Cultural Variations in Empathic Expression

Different cultures have varying norms around emotional expression, authority relationships, help-seeking behaviors, and conflict resolution. Some cultures prefer direct versus indirect communication of feelings, while others maintain hierarchical versus egalitarian interaction patterns. Individual versus collective approaches to problem-solving differ across cultures, as do confrontational versus harmony-preserving strategies.

Effective crisis empathy requires understanding these variations while maintaining core principles of validation, safety, and collaborative problem-solving.

Historical and Systemic Trauma Considerations

Many communities carry histories of collective trauma that influence their responses to crisis situations and authority figures. These histories may create additional barriers to trust-building that empathic leaders must acknowledge and address.

Understanding historical trauma contexts helps crisis leaders recognize when current behaviors reflect past experiences rather than present circumstances, avoid inadvertently replicating harmful patterns from previous crisis responses, build in additional time and support for trust-building processes, and engage community leaders and cultural liaisons as bridges to affected populations.

Building Empathic Capacity: Individual and Organizational Development

While empathy offers tremendous potential for transformative crisis management, realizing this potential requires intentional development at both individual and organizational levels. Empathic capacity doesn't emerge automatically, especially amid the pressure of crisis situations—it must be cultivated through deliberate practice, supportive structures, and ongoing reflection.

Individual Practices for Deepening Empathic Capacity

Mindfulness training, including meditation, conscious breathing, and present-moment awareness, develops the attentional control and emotional regulation that empathy requires. Research demonstrates that even brief mindfulness practices significantly enhance practitioners' ability to maintain presence and perspective amid emotional intensity (Siegel, 2012).

Systematic perspective-taking exercises develop the cognitive empathy that crisis management requires. Simple practices like "stakeholder chair" exercises or structured role-plays help leaders develop a more nuanced understanding of diverse viewpoints and experiences.

Regular reflection on crisis interactions—examining what worked, what didn't, and what patterns emerge—develops the self-awareness necessary for empathic rather than reactive crisis response.

Organizational Infrastructure for Empathic Crisis Management

Crisis response teams with diverse perspectives across functional areas, hierarchical levels, and social identities create structural support for empathic crisis management. Organizations can develop specific protocols that integrate empathic approaches into crisis response procedures, ensuring that relational considerations receive attention even amid pressure.

Expanding traditional after-action reviews to include examination of stakeholder experiences, relationship dynamics, and empathic effectiveness creates organizational learning about the human dimensions of crisis management.

Conclusion: The Transformative Promise of Crisis Empathy

The science of empathy in crisis response reveals why empathic approaches prove so effective: they work with rather than against fundamental human neurobiological and psychological needs for safety, connection, and understanding. By creating the conditions for nervous system regulation, cognitive flexibility, and collaborative engagement, empathy transforms crisis management from a damage-control exercise into an opportunity for meaningful change.

Understanding the neurobiological foundations of empathic connection—how it shifts brain states, activates social engagement systems, and creates psychological safety—provides crisis leaders with a scientific rationale for approaches that might otherwise seem "too soft" for crisis situations. The research is clear: empathy isn't just ethically preferable in crisis situations, it's strategically superior.

The barriers to empathic crisis management—time pressure, misconceptions about strength and weakness, fear of emotional contagion—prove surmountable when leaders understand both the science behind empathy and practical approaches for integrating it with necessary boundaries and technical responses.

As we'll explore in the next chapter, this scientific understanding creates the foundation for practical tools and approaches that translate empathic principles into effective crisis intervention strategies. The science of empathy provides the "why"—the next chapter provides the "how."

Empathy in Crisis Management

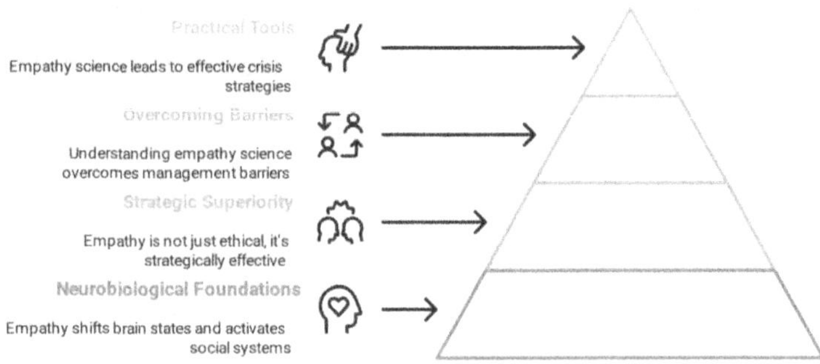

Questions for Personal Reflection or Group Discussion

Consider these questions individually or discuss with colleagues to deepen your understanding of empathy as a powerful neurobiological intervention.

Understanding Empathy in Practice

1. **Empathy vs. Agreement** Reflect on a situation where you successfully validated someone's perspective without agreeing with their conclusions or actions. How did this validation affect the interaction? How did it feel to maintain empathy while holding appropriate boundaries?
2. **Barriers to Empathy** What internal or external factors make it most difficult for you to maintain empathy during

crisis situations? How might understanding these barriers help you prepare for challenging interactions?

Application to Your Practice

3. **Creating Psychological Safety** Think about your work environment. What specific actions do you take that contribute to psychological safety for others? How do you balance empathy with necessary limits or consequences?
4. **Recognizing the "Yeah" Moment** Recall a time when you successfully created a moment of genuine connection with someone in distress. What did you notice in their response that indicated you had achieved true understanding? How did this moment change the trajectory of your interaction?

Systemic Reflection

5. **Organizational Empathy** How does your organization model empathic approaches in its policies and practices? What would it look like for your organization to systematically integrate empathy into crisis management protocols?

Integration Practice: During difficult conversations this week, focus on creating one genuine "yeah" moment before attempting problem-solving. Notice how this affects both the process and outcomes of your interactions.

References

Brown, B. (2018). *Dare to lead: Brave work, tough conversations, whole hearts*. Random House.

Edmondson, A. C. (1998). Psychological safety and learning behavior in work teams. *Administrative Science Quarterly*, 44(2), 350-383.

Edmondson, A. C. (2018). *The fearless organization: Creating psychological safety in the workplace for learning, innovation, and growth*. John Wiley & Sons.

LeDoux, J. E., & Pine, D. S. (2016). Using neuroscience to help understand fear and anxiety: A two-system framework. *American Journal of Psychiatry*, 173(11), 1083-1093.

Porges, S. W. (2011). *The polyvagal theory: Neurophysiological foundations of emotions, attachment, communication, and self-regulation*. W. W. Norton & Company.

Schore, A. N. (2003). *Affect dysregulation and disorders of the self*. W. W. Norton & Company.

Siegel, D. J. (2012). *The developing mind: How relationships and the brain interact to shape who we are* (2nd ed.). Guilford Press.

Taylor, S. E., Klein, L. C., Lewis, B. P., Gruenewald, T. L., Gurung, R. A. R., & Updegraff, J. A. (2000). Biobehavioral responses to stress in females: Tend-and-befriend, not fight-or-flight. *Psychological Review*, 107(3), 411-429.

van der Kolk, B. (2014). *The body keeps the score: Brain, mind, and body in the healing of trauma*. Viking.

Chapter 5: The Power of Human Connection - Evoking the "Yeah!"

Building on our understanding of neurobiological foundations and empathic crisis management, we now turn to a transformative concept that distills decades of neuroscience research into a simple yet powerful approach to conflict resolution: "Evoking the Yeah!"

Research in interpersonal neurobiology, as described by Daniel Siegel (2012), shows that attuned relationships allow our internal states to influence one another, fostering deep connection and mutual understanding. This chapter explores how focusing our efforts on eliciting genuine moments of openness and engagement harnesses the power of human connection to create profound shifts in the emotional landscape of any interaction.

The "yeah" moment represents that pivotal response where an individual feels truly seen, heard, and understood. It's a palpable shift in their demeanor—a softening of expression or change in posture that indicates they have made a meaningful connection with you. This moment signifies more than cognitive acknowledgment; it represents a whole-body state change that creates the foundation for meaningful dialogue and resolution.

The Neurobiology of the "Yeah" Moment

Neuroscience research has consistently shown that when individuals connect on a deep, empathic level, their neural activity begins to synchronize. This synchronization fosters feelings of safety and trust, which are essential for de-escalation (Gallese, 2001). Dr. Stephen Porges' Polyvagal Theory offers crucial insight into this phenomenon. When we feel threatened, our nervous system shifts into a sympathetic "fight-or-flight" state or, in extreme cases, a dorsal vagal "freeze" response. These states inhibit our ability to connect, reason, and collaborate. However, when we experience authentic connection—when someone truly sees and hears us—our nervous system can shift into a ventral vagal state of safety and social engagement (Porges, 2017).

Research by Dr. Uri Hasson on "neural coupling" demonstrates that during effective communication, the brain activity of the speaker and listener actually begins to mirror each other. This neural synchrony creates a shared mental model that facilitates deeper understanding and cooperation. When we evoke the "yeah," we're essentially creating the conditions for this neural coupling to occur, allowing for a genuine meeting of minds (Hasson et al., 2012).

The neurobiological underpinnings of the "yeah" moment include several key processes. Porges' term "neuroception" describes how our nervous system continuously evaluates risk without conscious awareness. When we successfully evoke the "yeah," we're changing someone's neuroception from perceiving threat to perceiving safety—fundamental to moving from defensive reactions to collaborative engagement.

When people feel threatened, blood flow decreases to their prefrontal cortex—the brain region responsible for rational thinking and problem-solving. The "yeah" moment reverses this process, re-engaging the prefrontal cortex and enhancing executive function. This is why people who feel genuinely understood suddenly become more reasonable, creative, and solution-focused (Arnsten, 2015).

Conflict triggers stress hormones like cortisol and adrenaline. The experience of being truly heard counters this process, reducing stress hormone levels and activating the parasympathetic nervous system—our "rest and digest" mode that allows for thoughtful, measured responses (Sapolsky, 2004). These neurochemicals not only create immediate positive feelings but also support the growth of new neural connections, enhancing resilience over time (Siegel, 2012).

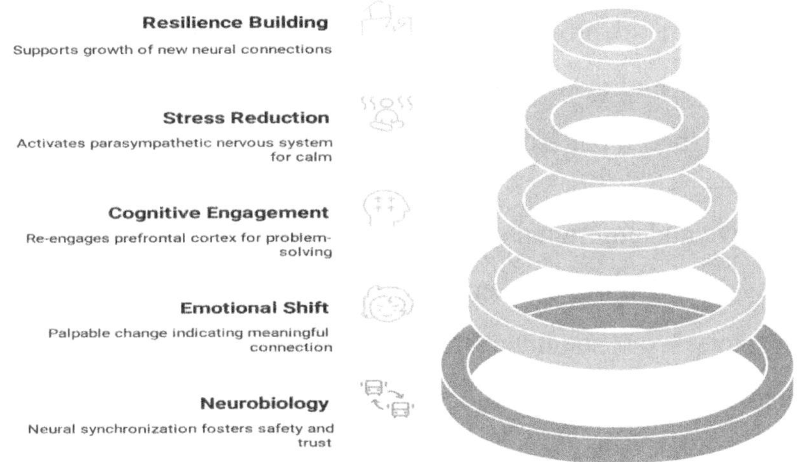

Recognizing the "Yeah" Moment

Learning to recognize these pivotal moments becomes an essential skill for anyone seeking to navigate conflict effectively. The "yeah" moment can be subtle or dramatic, but it always represents a shift from defensive posture to openness (Dana, 2018). The "yeah" moment often presents through observable physical changes. There's typically a "settling" of the body, with shoulders dropping or releasing tension, deeper and more relaxed breathing patterns, facial tension releasing with softer expressions, a slight forward lean indicating engagement rather than defensiveness, and unclenched fists or relaxed hand positions.

Vocal changes accompany these physical shifts as tone shifts from tense or sharp to more receptive and warm, speaking pace slows down from rapid, anxious speech, volume moderates from either very quiet withdrawal or loud defensiveness, and breathing spaces appear in speech patterns.

Cognitive and emotional shifts become apparent as the person moves from defensive statements to exploratory ones, shifts from accusatory "you" statements to reflective "I" statements, shows increased willingness to volunteer information or share vulnerabilities, asks questions that show curiosity rather than challenge, and begins acknowledging other perspectives.

Relational opening manifests through increased eye contact or appropriate gaze engagement, body position opening up rather than turning away, willingness to engage in back-and-forth dialogue, reduced interrupting or talking over others, and collaborative language using words like "we," "together," and "how can we."

Sometimes it's literally hearing the word "yeah" spoken with a tone of relief and recognition—"Yeah, that's exactly how I feel" or "Yeah, you get it." Other times, it might be a long exhale followed by "I never thought about it that way." These indicators signal that the person has moved from a defensive posture to one of openness—a neurological state shift that creates the possibility for collaborative problem-solving.

The Power of Co-regulation

Central to evoking the "yeah" moment is the process of co-regulation. This concept, with roots in early developmental psychology and attachment, helps explain why connection is so powerful in moments of conflict.

Co-regulation operates through multiple channels, beginning with physiological synchrony. When we are in the presence of a calm, regulated person, our bodies naturally begin to match their physiological state—our breathing slows, our heart rate decreases, and our muscle tension diminishes. This biological synchrony occurs below conscious awareness and creates the physiological foundation for the "yeah" moment (Feldman, 2007).

Through facial expressions, vocal tone, gestures, and posture, we continually communicate our internal state to others. A regulated person sends consistent signals of safety that help dysregulated individuals recalibrate their own nervous systems. These non-verbal cues often matter more than our actual words in creating conditions for connection.

Rhythmic interactions—the natural give-and-take of conversation, synchronized movements, or even breathing together—create a shared regulatory experience that helps stabilize a dysregulated nervous system. This explains why sometimes simply sitting with someone in quiet presence can be more effective than elaborate verbal interventions (Perry, 2020).

When we understand Co-regulation, we realize that "evoking the yeah" is not just about saying the right words—it's about bringing a regulated presence that helps the other person's nervous system shift toward safety and connection.

Recognizing and evoking "Yeah" moments through coregulation leads to collaborative problem-solving.

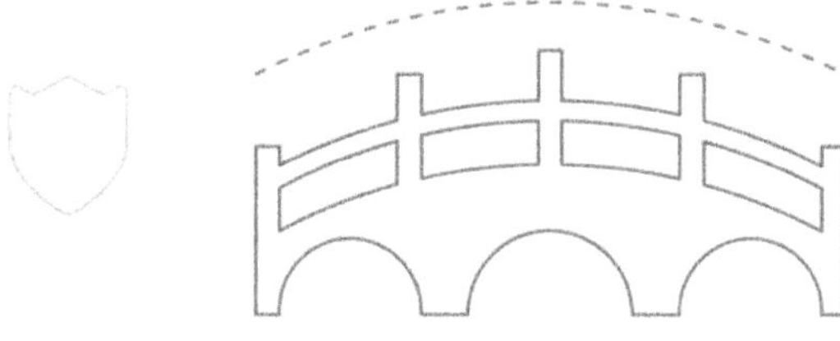

Conflict & defensiveness

Individuals are in defensive postures.

Openness & collaboration

Individuals are open to collaborative problem-solving.

Creating the Conditions for Connection

To consistently evoke the "yeah" response, we need to develop specific skills and mindsets that create safe spaces for authentic dialogue. Essential connection skills begin with presence—bringing your full attention to the interaction, setting aside distractions, agendas, and preconceptions. This means being genuinely available in the moment rather than thinking about what you'll say next (Siegel, 2010).

Authentic curiosity involves approaching the other person with genuine interest in their experience, without assumptions about what they "should" be feeling or thinking. This curiosity communicates respect for their perspective and creates space for them to share authentically (Rosenberg, 2015).

Reflective listening goes beyond simply hearing words to reflecting back the emotional content and underlying meaning of what's being expressed. This helps the person feel understood at a deeper level than just the surface content (Miller & Rollnick, 2012).

Validation acknowledges the legitimacy of the other person's feelings and perspective, even when you don't agree with their conclusions or actions. Validation creates psychological safety by communicating that their emotions make sense given their experience (Linehan, 2014).

Self-regulation involves managing your own emotional responses so you can remain present and connected even when triggered. This is fundamental to offering coregulatory support to others (Van der Kolk, 2014). Patience allows the necessary time and space for the other person to process and respond, without rushing to solutions. Transformation takes time, and the "yeah" moment cannot be forced.

The Foundation: Introducing the Four-Step Framework

While the "yeah" moment can occur spontaneously, we can create systematic approaches to increase the likelihood of authentic connection. The MindSet Four-Step Model provides a structured pathway for building these moments of understanding through Acknowledgment, Acceptance, Validation, and Empowerment.

These four steps provide the practical structure for creating the conditions where "yeah" moments naturally emerge. Each step builds on the previous one, creating a progression from surface-level observation to deeper understanding and ultimately to collaborative action. This framework represents the integration of all the neurobiological and empathic principles we've explored—translating brain science into practical tools for transformation.

This framework will be explored in comprehensive detail in Chapter 6, where we'll examine how to maintain and deepen these connections through sustained dialogue and complex conflicts. The power of this framework lies not in rigid application, but in how it creates space for authentic human connection. When we learn to see without judgment, accept emotional realities, validate experiences, and empower choice, we create the neurobiological conditions necessary for genuine transformation.

The "Yeah" Moment in Action: Scotty's Story

To illustrate the profound power of evoking authentic connection, let's examine a moment that captures the essence of transformative crisis management—a scene that reveals the delicate art of seeing beyond behavior to the human experience underneath.

The fluorescent lights buzzed overhead, a constant drone that matched the low-level anxiety always humming beneath Scotty's skin. Fifth grade had become a battlefield, and he was losing ground every single day. His desk sat perpetually messy, a topography of crumpled worksheets and broken pencils that mirrored the chaos inside his head. ADHD, they said. Emotional behavioral disorder, the reports claimed. But what those clinical terms really meant was simple: Scotty felt everything too big, too loud, too intense.

That morning started like most others. The math worksheet landed on his desk—another maze of numbers that refused to make sense. The letters danced, shifted, mocked him. His fingers gripped the pencil so tightly his knuckles turned white, then released, sending the pencil skittering across the floor. Mrs. Hendricks's voice cut through his spiral. "Scotty, pick that up. NOW!" The word "now" landed like a slap. His ears burned. His chest tightened. The classroom—with its neat rows, its silent students, its suffocating expectations—suddenly felt impossibly small.

"I can't do this," he muttered. "What did you say?" Mrs. Hendricks's voice rose, that edge of frustration he knew too well creeping in. Something inside Scotty snapped. He was up, pushing his desk away—his body the only weapon he knew how to wield. Words became missiles. Anger became language. Frustration became movement. He was yelling now, hands raised, fists clenched tight—the universal signal of a child who has run out of ways to be heard.

Mrs. Hendricks yelled back, her composure shattered. Spittle flew. Threats emerged. But Scotty couldn't hear the words anymore. He could only feel the overwhelming sense of being wrong. Always wrong.

The Intervention: Connection in Practice

And then someone else entered. Calm. Different. The intervention wasn't like anything Scotty had experienced before. No immediate punishment. No instant dismissal. Just acknowledgment. Just listening.

The first step involved neutral observation without judgment. "I hear you are yelling, and it seems like you are frustrated and in need of a break," the newcomer said to Mrs. Hendricks. Then, turning to Scotty: "I see you standing near your desk while yelling at your teacher. Your hands are clenched tight. You are very angry." These were simple words that carried powerful recognition. No judgment, just observation.

When everyone else had left and he was alone with this calm presence, Scotty's bravado crumbled. "Yeah, that bitch won't listen to me," he muttered, the curse word a last-ditch attempt at maintaining his defensive wall.

The second step focused on recognition of underlying emotional states. The response came without judgment: "Yeah, it's hard when you have something to say and nobody wants to give you the time to say it."

In that instant, something shifted. This was the "Yeah" Moment. Scotty's shoulders dropped slightly. His breathing deepened. For the first time in longer than he could remember, he felt seen. Not fixed. Not judged. Just seen. "Yeah," he whispered, and in that simple word was recognition, relief, and the beginning of connection. The desk beneath him felt solid. His breathing slowed. And for just a moment, the chaos inside him quieted to a manageable hum.

This story exemplifies how the "yeah" moment emerges naturally when we create the right conditions. The intervenor remained calm despite Scotty's intense dysregulation, providing a coregulatory resource. Rather than immediately correcting or controlling, the response began with pure acknowledgment of what was observable. The intervention recognized and accepted Scotty's underlying emotional state without trying to change it immediately. Scotty's feelings were validated without endorsing his disrespectful language or behavior. The "yeah" emerged naturally because Scotty felt safe enough to be genuine rather than defensive.

This is the essence of transformative crisis management—not controlling behavior, but understanding the human experience beneath it. The "yeah" moment signaled that Scotty's nervous system had shifted from a defensive state to one of connection, creating the foundation for everything that followed.

Barriers to Evoking the "Yeah"

Despite its power, several common obstacles can prevent us from successfully evoking moments of authentic connection. Internal barriers often emerge from our own triggers. When someone's behavior activates our own trauma responses or challenges deeply held values, we may struggle to remain present and curious. Recognizing our triggers is the first step to managing them effectively.

Being overly attached to a specific resolution can prevent us from truly listening and connecting. When we're focused on where we want the conversation to go, we miss opportunities to meet the person where they are. Feeling rushed often leads us to skip the connection phase and move directly to problem-solving, undermining the very foundation that makes solutions possible.

External barriers include severe dysregulation, where some individuals may be so physiologically dysregulated that they need safety and co-regulation before meaningful connection can occur. In these cases, patient presence becomes more important than words. Noisy, chaotic, or public environments can make it difficult to create the conditions for vulnerable sharing. Sometimes changing the setting is necessary before connection can happen.

Significant power imbalances may require additional trust-building before authentic connection becomes possible. This is particularly important in hierarchical relationships. Different cultural norms around emotional expression and conflict resolution may require adapted approaches to connection while maintaining core principles of respect and understanding.

Developing Your Connection Skills

Like any skill, evoking the "yeah" moment requires deliberate practice. Self-regulation practices begin with the three-breath reset. Before entering a potentially difficult conversation, take your first breath to notice any tension or reactivity in your body, your second breath to recall your intention to connect rather than control, and your third breath to imagine yourself fully present and receptive.

This brief reset helps shift your nervous system into a state conducive to connection. Remember that effective co-regulation begins with self-regulation—you cannot offer regulatory presence to others if you're dysregulated yourself.

Coregulatory presence practice involves maintaining a regulatory presence during interactions by keeping your breathing deep and steady, even when the other person is agitated, maintaining a relaxed facial expression and open body language, speaking in a calm, even tone with a rhythm that naturally slows rapid speech, and creating appropriate moments of silence that allow for integration.

Connection skills development includes neutral observation practice, where you practice describing what you see without interpretation. Say things like "I notice your voice is louder than usual," "I see you've moved away from the group," or "Your hands are moving quickly as you speak." Develop curiosity questions that demonstrate genuine interest rather than judgment, such as "What's been most challenging about this for you?" "How has this situation been affecting you?" or "What would be most helpful for you right now?"

Advanced practices include enhancing your ability to recognize subtle signs of the "yeah" moment by studying facial expressions, body language, and vocal tone changes that indicate shifts from defensiveness to openness. After each significant interaction, reflect on whether you successfully created conditions for a "yeah" moment, what internal or external barriers were present, and what you might try differently next time. This reflective practice accelerates learning and helps internalize the principles of effective connection.

The Integration of Connection and Co-regulation

The "Evoking the Yeah" principle represents the integration of meaningful understanding with physiological co-regulation. According to Polyvagal Theory (Porges, 2011), our nervous system is continuously evaluating environmental cues for safety, and when we feel safe, we can access our social engagement system—the neurobiological state most conducive to connection and collaboration.

This biological foundation—the capacity to help another's nervous system feel safe through our regulated presence—makes the "yeah" moment much more than a communication technique. It's a profound biological gift we can offer one another.

When we successfully integrate connection and co-regulation, we create what research in interpersonal neurobiology describes as "resonance circuits"—neural pathways that allow our brains to attune deeply to others' experiences. These resonance circuits enable the empathy, understanding, and collaborative problem-solving that define successful conflict resolution (Siegel, 2012).

Beyond Connection: Opening Doors to Transformation

At its highest level, evoking the "yeah" moment becomes more than relationship-building—it becomes an opportunity for mutual transformation. When we create authentic moments of connection, we open doors to expanded awareness, where both parties develop deeper understanding of themselves and others. We build increased resilience, as everyone involved develops greater capacity for handling future challenges. We enhance trust, as successfully creating connection strengthens relational bonds. We access collective wisdom, as insights emerge that neither person could have accessed alone.

This transformative potential makes the investment in connection skills worthwhile—it creates outcomes that couldn't have been predicted or designed by any single perspective.

Conclusion: The Heart of Human Connection

The "yeah" moment represents the intersection of science and humanity, where neurobiological understanding meets the profound human need to be seen and understood. By learning to create these moments of authentic connection, we tap into one of our most powerful tools for transformation.

This approach requires us to shift from trying to control outcomes to creating conditions for connection. It asks us to slow down enough to truly see and hear one another, to offer our regulated presence as a gift, and to trust in the wisdom that emerges when people feel genuinely understood.

The "yeah" moment is both a destination and a beginning—a moment of recognition that opens the door to everything that follows. By mastering the art and science of connection, we create the foundation for all transformative work that follows.

These moments of connection—the "Yeah!"—open the door to transformation. But sustaining that connection through difficult conversations and complex conflicts requires additional skills, structured approaches, and practical frameworks. In our next chapter, we'll explore how to maintain and deepen these connections through the most challenging dialogues life presents us.

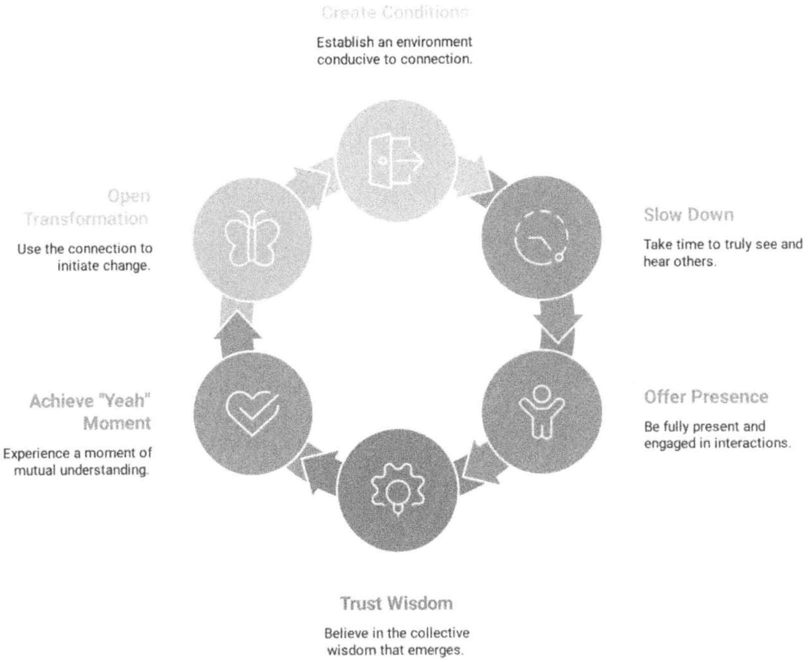

Questions for Personal Reflection or Group Discussion

Consider these questions individually or discuss with colleagues to deepen your understanding of creating authentic moments of connection.

Understanding Connection

1. **Recognizing Your Connection Style** Reflect on how you typically try to connect with others during difficult

moments. Do you tend to focus more on problem-solving, emotional support, or providing information? How might expanding your approach create deeper connections?

2. **Self-Regulation and Presence** Think about your capacity to remain present and regulated when others are dysregulated. What helps you maintain the calm, centered presence necessary for effective co-regulation?

Application to Your Practice

3. **Creating Safety for Authenticity** Consider someone in your care who tends to be guarded or defensive. What might need to change in your approach or environment to help them feel safe enough to be genuine rather than protective?
4. **Cultural Considerations in Connection** How might different cultural backgrounds affect what "connection" looks and feels like? How can you adapt your approach to honor diverse communication styles while maintaining authentic engagement?

Systemic Reflection

5. **Organizational Connection Culture** Evaluate how your organization supports or hinders authentic connection between staff and those they serve. What structural changes

would create more opportunities for meaningful relationship-building?

Integration Practice: This week, practice neutral observation with someone showing signs of distress. Simply reflect what you see without trying to fix or change anything. Notice how this affects their response and your relationship.

References

Arnsten, A. F. T. (2015). Stress weakens prefrontal networks: Molecular insults to higher cognition. *Nature Neuroscience*, 18(10), 1376-1385. https://doi.org/10.1038/nn.4087

Dana, D. (2018). *The polyvagal theory in therapy: Engaging the rhythm of regulation*. W. W. Norton & Company.

Feldman, R. (2007). Parent-infant synchrony and the construction of shared timing: Physiological precursors, developmental outcomes, and risk conditions. *Journal of Child Psychology and Psychiatry*, 48(3-4), 329-354. https://doi.org/10.1111/j.1469-7610.2006.01701.x

Gallese, V. (2001). The shared manifold hypothesis: From mirror neurons to empathy. *Journal of Consciousness Studies*, 8(5-6), 33-50.

Hasson, U., Ghazanfar, A. A., Galantucci, B., Garrod, S., & Keysers, C. (2012). Brain-to-brain coupling: A mechanism for creating and sharing a social world. *Trends in Cognitive Sciences*, 16(2), 114-121. https://doi.org/10.1016/j.tics.2011.12.007

Linehan, M. M. (2014). *DBT skills training manual* (2nd ed.). Guilford Press.

Miller, W. R., & Rollnick, S. (2012). *Motivational interviewing: Helping people change* (3rd ed.). Guilford Press.

Perry, B. D. (2020). *What happened to you? Conversations on trauma, resilience, and healing*. Flatiron Books.

Porges, S. W. (2017). *The pocket guide to the polyvagal theory: The transformative power of feeling safe*. W. W. Norton & Company.

Rosenberg, M. B. (2015). *Nonviolent communication: A language of life* (3rd ed.). PuddleDancer Press.

Sapolsky, R. M. (2004). *Why zebras don't get ulcers* (3rd ed.). Holt Paperbacks.

Siegel, D. J. (2010). *Mindsight: The new science of personal transformation*. Bantam.

Siegel, D. J. (2012). *The developing mind: How relationships and the brain interact to shape who we are* (2nd ed.). Guilford Press.

van der Kolk, B. (2014). *The body keeps the score: Brain, mind, and body in the healing of trauma*. Viking.

Chapter 6: From Connection to Sustained Dialogue - Navigating Difficult Conversations

Creating moments of connection is powerful, but sustaining that connection through ongoing challenges requires additional skills. This chapter explores how to maintain empathic relationships through difficult conversations, building on our understanding of nervous system states and the power of authentic connection to navigate complex conflicts with grace and skill.

Our exploration of evoking the "yeah" moment has shown us how to create those crucial instances of connection that open the door to transformation. Now we turn to the equally important challenge of sustaining and deepening these connections through the skilled navigation of difficult conversations.

The art of managing challenging dialogues builds directly upon our understanding of nervous system states and the power of authentic connection. When we recognize that every conversation carries the potential for either deepening trust or triggering defensive responses, we can approach these interactions with greater wisdom and skill.

In the bustling corridors of our schools and the intimate spaces of our homes, conflict is as inevitable as the changing seasons and as intrinsic to human interaction as breathing. As Coleman and colleagues (2014) note in their comprehensive handbook on conflict resolution, whether you're an educator navigating the complex social ecology of a classroom or a parent mediating a sibling squabble, developing the skills to engage with conflict productively has the power to transform challenges into opportunities for growth, learning, and the strengthening of relational bonds.

This chapter explores how to maintain connection even as we address challenging topics, moving beyond simple conflict resolution toward conversations that transform all participants. The goal is not to eliminate conflict but to harness its potential as a catalyst for deeper understanding and stronger relationships.

The Four-Step MindSet Model: From Theory to Practice

Understanding the brain science of connection is crucial, but how does this translate to the moment someone is struggling right in front of you? The MindSet Four-Step Model offers a structured approach to connecting with individuals navigating difficult circumstances. Rooted in neuroscience, this model translates scientific principles into practical strategies that anyone can learn and apply.

The model recognizes a key insight that people deeply engaged in a problem-solving conversation are typically focused on their own perceptions and agenda, desperately attempting to convince the other person that they are justified. This often leads to power struggles. The MindSet model offers an alternative approach that views conflict as an opportunity to strengthen relationships.

The model's success lies in remaining calm and communicating with empathy. As research emphasizes, the path of empathy leads toward empowerment and connection, whereas the path of demanding compliance leads toward resistance and separation. This fundamental choice between empathy and control shapes every interaction and determines whether conflicts escalate or transform into opportunities for deeper understanding.

The Four-Step MindSet Model: Quick Reference

While each step will be explored in detail, this quick reference provides the essential framework:

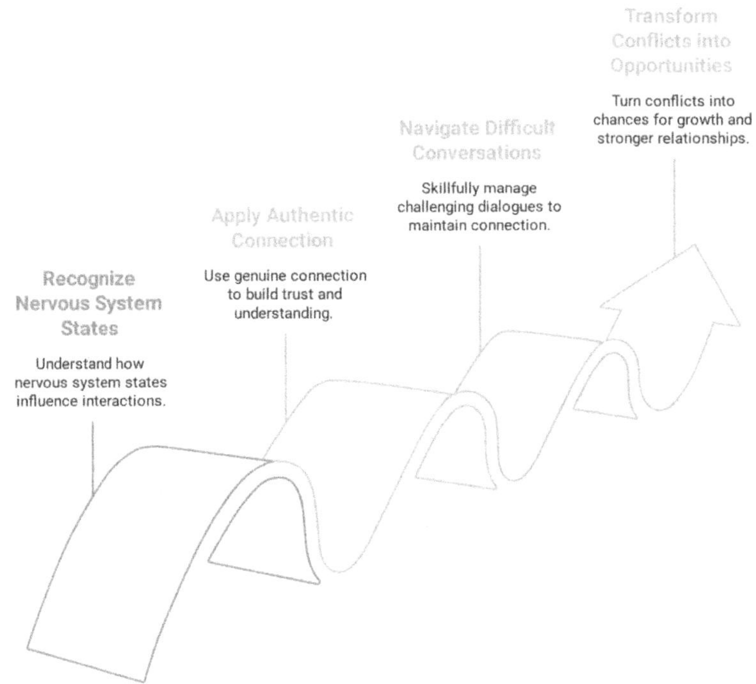

Step 1: Acknowledgment – "I See You"

- Notice and name what is observable without judgment
- Create a neurological reset from reactive to responsive
- Example: "I notice you're tapping your foot frequently"

Step 2: Acceptance – Understanding Emotional Drivers

- Recognize and validate the emotional state driving behavior
- Move from behavior focus to emotional awareness

- Example: "It seems like you might be feeling frustrated about this assignment"

Step 3: Validation – Honoring Perception Without Agreement

- Acknowledge legitimacy of someone's perception without agreeing
- Normalize emotional reactions and reduce shame
- Example: "It makes sense that you'd feel overwhelmed given what you're experiencing"

Step 4: Empowerment – Fostering Agency and Dignity

- Support individuals in making decisions that address the situation
- Honor humanity and dignity through meaningful choice
- Example: "What do you think would help resolve this situation?"

Step 1: Acknowledgment – "I See You"

The first step centers on staying fully present and engaged without judgment. This present-moment awareness helps activate the part of our nervous system associated with social engagement and connection. When we remain calm and grounded, our regulated state offers dysregulated individuals a chance to begin stabilizing their own nervous systems through the process of co-regulation.

In practice, acknowledgment means noticing and naming what is observable without adding judgment or interpretation. This might sound like "I notice you're tapping your foot frequently," "Your voice sounds different than it did earlier," "I see you've put your head down on your desk," or "I observe that you stepped away when we started discussing the deadline." The power of acknowledgment lies in its ability to interrupt common escalation patterns. When adults immediately correct or impose consequences, they often reinforce the person's perception of being under threat. In contrast, neutral acknowledgment creates a critical pause—a neurological reset button that helps shift both parties from reactive to responsive modes.

The neuroscience behind this step leverages what research in interpersonal neurobiology describes as "name it to tame it"—the process by which labeling experiences helps regulate the amygdala and activate the prefrontal cortex (Siegel, 2012). When we acknowledge without judgment, we help the other person move from emotional reactivity to reflective awareness. This simple act of neutral observation communicates that we are paying attention and that their experience matters, without immediately trying to change or fix anything.

Step 2: Acceptance – Understanding Emotional Drivers

The second step focuses on recognizing and validating the emotional state driving the behavior. Research shows that affect labeling—putting feelings into words—reduces emotional reactivity and increases activity in areas supporting more adaptive responses (Lieberman et al., 2007). For trauma-impacted individuals, emotions may exist primarily as implicit, body-based memories. The acceptance step helps move these experiences from the "downstairs brain" (limbic system) to the "upstairs brain" (prefrontal cortex) where they can be processed more adaptively.

This step might sound like "It seems like you might be feeling frustrated about this assignment," "I'm wondering if you're feeling overwhelmed by everything happening right now," "It appears you might be experiencing anxiety about the upcoming changes," or "I imagine you could be feeling disappointed by how this turned out." The key is to offer these observations tentatively, recognizing that our initial assessment may be incorrect, but this still moves the process forward constructively.

If your assessment is wrong, this creates an opportunity for the person to clarify their actual emotional state. For example, if someone responds "No, I'm not frustrated" to your observation, you might reply "I hear you—help me understand. What are you feeling right now?" This exchange still accomplishes the goal of moving from behavior focus to emotional awareness, which is essential for meaningful resolution.

The acceptance step acknowledges that emotions are valid responses to perceived circumstances, even when the perception may be distorted by past experiences or current stressors. This recognition creates space for the person to begin understanding their own emotional experience without feeling judged or pathologized for having natural human responses to challenging situations.

Step 3: Validation – Honoring Perception Without Agreement

The third step focuses on validation—acknowledging the legitimacy of someone's perception without necessarily agreeing with it. This distinction is crucial because validation reduces emotional reactivity and creates space for more adaptive problem-solving, even when the helper doesn't endorse the person's interpretation of events.

A key understanding here is that the individual's perception could be based in private logic influenced by past experiences and various factors—their perception is true for them. Therefore, it is counterproductive to try to convince them that they are wrong about their own experience. This is where empathy resides within the model. To have genuine empathy, we must connect with something within ourselves that can identify with their feelings.

Research demonstrates that validation significantly reduces individuals' "belonging uncertainty"—concerns about whether they would be accepted and respected (Walton & Cohen, 2007). This step might sound like "That sounds really disappointing," "I can understand why you'd feel that way," "It makes sense that you're upset about that," "Given what you've experienced, it's completely understandable that you'd feel overwhelmed," or "Anyone facing these circumstances would likely feel frustrated."

The power of validation lies in its ability to normalize emotional reactions that individuals may be judging harshly in themselves. During crises, people often struggle not just with the situation itself but with their own reactions to it—feeling weak for being scared, guilty for being angry, or ashamed for feeling overwhelmed. Validation interrupts this secondary layer of distress by communicating that their emotional response makes sense given their circumstances.

Importantly, validation doesn't require agreement with the person's actions or conclusions. We can validate that someone feels betrayed without agreeing that betrayal occurred. We can validate that someone feels unsafe without accepting that danger is present. This distinction allows helpers to maintain appropriate boundaries while still providing emotional support and creating the psychological safety necessary for productive dialogue.

Step 4: Empowerment – Fostering Agency and Dignity

The final step focuses on empowerment—supporting individuals in making decisions that address the situation. This emphasis on empowerment aligns with research showing that when people have meaningful choices, they show greater engagement, persistence, and learning (Deci & Ryan, 2000). The ability to make decisions leads to empowerment, and leaving the decision with the individual honors the humanity and dignity of the individual by providing them the chance to self-advocate.

The challenge lies in avoiding providing a way out and being okay with choices that aren't necessarily optimal. However, the decision must be acceptable to both parties, highlighting the collaborative nature of effective problem-solving. This step might sound like "What do you think would help resolve this situation?" "What are some options you're considering?" "How do you want to handle this moving forward?" "What would need to happen for you to feel more confident about this?" or "You've handled difficult situations before—what worked for you then?"

True empowerment involves supporting someone's capacity to make good decisions within appropriate constraints. It's not about removing all consequences or boundaries, but about ensuring the person maintains agency within realistic limits. This approach recognizes that people are more likely to follow through on solutions they've helped create and that the process of making meaningful choices builds confidence and self-efficacy over time.

The empowerment step also acknowledges that individuals often have insights into their own situations that others might miss. By genuinely seeking their input and respecting their agency, we tap into their own wisdom and problem-solving capacity while building their sense of competence and autonomy.

Seeing the Model in Action: Fredrick's Story

To illustrate how the Four-Step Model works in sustained dialogue, let's follow a more complex scenario that unfolds over time—demonstrating how initial connection can be maintained through ongoing challenges and how the relationship itself becomes a resource for navigating difficulties.

It's Tuesday morning in Ms. Peterson's high school English class when Fredrick, a sophomore, drops his head into his hands and mutters "I'm so screwed" as she announces that final projects are due at the end of class. Several students around him are putting finishing touches on their week-long literature analysis projects while his remains only half-completed. As one classmate confidently submits his project, Fredrick looks at him and says bitterly, "Sure, it's easy for you."

In the past, this might have led to a reprimand for his snarky response or a consequence for not meeting expectations. Instead, Ms. Peterson applies the MindSet model with genuine curiosity about what might be happening for Fredrick. She approaches him with acknowledgment: "Fredrick, I notice you put your head down when I mentioned the deadline, and I heard you say something under your breath." This is pure observation without judgment, simply naming what she witnessed.

Moving to acceptance, she continues: "It seems like the project deadline might be causing you some stress right now." This invites Fredrick to share more about his internal experience rather than defending his behavior. His response reveals the complexity beneath his apparent lack of preparation: "I got started last week but couldn't finish! My grandmother had surgery this past weekend and my mom's been staying with her at the hospital. I've been home taking care of my little brother and sister, and now I'm afraid I might lose my job because I missed three shifts!"

Ms. Peterson moves to validation, recognizing the enormous challenges Fredrick is facing: "That sounds incredibly overwhelming. You clearly put effort into starting this project, and then life threw you this enormous challenge. Being responsible for your siblings while your mom cares for your grandmother, plus worrying about your job—that's an enormous amount of stress for anyone to handle. It makes complete sense that finishing schoolwork would feel impossible right now."

Finally, she offers empowerment: "What do you think might help you move forward with this? Do you want to talk about a modified timeline, or would it help to connect with some resources that might support you during this difficult time?" This approach honors Fredrick's autonomy while offering genuine support and recognizing that he's dealing with real-life circumstances that require flexibility and understanding.

The Follow-Up Conversation

The interaction doesn't end there, demonstrating how sustained dialogue requires maintaining the relational foundation through ongoing complexity. Fredrick chooses to discuss a brief extension with a clear plan for completion, and Ms. Peterson helps him connect with the school counselor for additional family support resources. But this is where sustained dialogue becomes crucial—maintaining the connection through the ongoing challenges rather than considering the problem solved after one conversation.

Three days later, Fredrick approaches Ms. Peterson after class, demonstrating that the initial connection created safety for him to continue seeking support: "Ms. Peterson, I'm still struggling. My grandmother came home from the hospital but she needs a lot of help, and my mom is exhausted. I started the project again but I don't think I'm going to make even the extended deadline."

Rather than moving immediately to problem-solving or expressing frustration about the ongoing challenges, Ms. Peterson maintains the relational foundation by applying the four-step model again. She begins with acknowledgment: "I see you're coming to me proactively about this challenge, and I hear the stress in your voice." This recognizes his responsibility in seeking help while acknowledging his ongoing distress.

She continues with acceptance: "It sounds like you're feeling caught between wanting to succeed in school and needing to support your family." This captures the internal conflict he's experiencing rather than focusing only on the academic issue. Moving to validation, she says: "This is such a difficult position to be in. You're showing real maturity by balancing these responsibilities, and it makes sense that you'd feel torn. Many adults would struggle with what you're managing right now."

Finally, she offers empowerment: "You've been thinking about this situation—what feels like it might work best for you? And what kind of support would help you manage both your family needs and your academic goals?" This approach maintains his agency while recognizing the complexity of his circumstances and offering collaborative problem-solving.

This extended example illustrates several key principles of sustained dialogue. Even when time pressures exist, maintaining the relational foundation actually speeds up problem-solving by preventing escalation and resistance. Each new conversation requires fresh validation, not just reference to previous understanding. As situations develop, new choiccs and options may emerge that weren't available initially. Each successful application of the Four-Step Model builds trust for future interactions, making subsequent conversations easier and more productive.

The Dialogue Continuum: Understanding Conversation Complexity

Difficult conversations exist on a continuum, from mild disagreements to high-stakes conflicts. Understanding where your conversation falls on this spectrum helps you calibrate your approach appropriately and recognize when additional skills or resources might be needed.

At the simplest level are clarification conversations—simple misunderstandings that require information sharing and perspective-taking. An example might be "I thought the meeting was at 2:00, but you said 3:00." The approach focuses on information exchange and mutual understanding, often resolved quickly once the miscommunication is identified.

Collaboration conversations involve working through differences to reach a mutual goal, such as team members with different approaches to the same project. The approach emphasizes shared objectives while exploring different methods, recognizing that multiple valid approaches might exist and seeking to integrate the best elements of each.

Negotiation conversations address competing interests to find acceptable compromises, such as budget allocation decisions where departments have different priorities. The approach focuses on underlying needs rather than stated positions, seeking creative solutions that address core concerns for all parties involved.

Mediation conversations involve navigating significant conflicts that require structured process and possibly third-party assistance, such as long-standing workplace conflicts affecting multiple people. The approach uses formal conflict resolution processes while maintaining relationship focus, often requiring neutral facilitation to help parties communicate effectively.

At the most complex level are reconciliation conversations—healing deep relational ruptures caused by serious breaches of trust or harm, such as rebuilding relationships after betrayal or significant harm. The approach focuses on accountability, repair, and rebuilding trust over time, recognizing that healing from serious harm requires sustained commitment and often professional support.

Each level requires increasingly sophisticated conversational skills, all built on the foundation of connection established through the four-step model. Understanding this continuum helps practitioners recognize when they might need additional support or when the conversation might benefit from a more structured approach.

Advanced Applications of the Four-Step Model in Complex Dialogues

When facilitating group conversations, acknowledgment becomes like being a conductor who needs to be aware of every instrument in the orchestra. You might say something like "I'm noticing we've got some really different perspectives in the room right now. Sarah, you've been pretty quiet since we started talking about the budget. Mark, I see you've kind of pulled back in your chair. And Jennifer, your voice has gotten more intense as we've been discussing this." This comprehensive acknowledgment helps everyone feel seen while mapping the emotional landscape of the group.

Holding space for multiple emotional realities becomes essential when you've got several people in a room, as you're probably dealing with several different emotional experiences happening simultaneously. You might observe: "It seems like there might be a few different things happening right now. Some people might be frustrated that we're going over this again. Others could be feeling anxious about moving too fast. And I'm sensing some folks feel like they haven't been heard in previous conversations about this." This approach validates the complexity of group dynamics while avoiding oversimplification.

Validation gets particularly tricky in groups because you need to honor different perspectives without making anyone feel like you're playing favorites. You might say: "Everyone here is trying to figure out how to balance things we all care about—keeping students safe, encouraging innovation, and working within our resource constraints. These aren't easy tensions to navigate, and there aren't simple answers." This type of validation acknowledges the legitimate concerns of different stakeholders while avoiding taking sides.

De-escalation and Repair Techniques

Even with skillful application of the four-step model, conversations sometimes go off track. Recognizing when connection is lost becomes crucial for effective intervention. Warning signs include sudden shifts in body language, people starting to defend positions instead of exploring solutions, someone who was engaged suddenly checking out, language becoming competitive rather than collaborative, curiosity disappearing as people dig into corners, voices getting louder or more intense, and multiple people talking at once.

When these warning signs appear, immediate repair strategies can help restore connection. You might pause the conversation and say: "I notice the energy in our conversation just changed. Can we pause and check in about what's happening?" or "I think I might have said something that didn't land well. Can someone help me understand what I missed?" or "It feels like we've shifted from exploring this together to defending positions. What happened that we should pay attention to?"

Sometimes process adjustments are needed to restore productive dialogue. You might ask: "What would help us have this conversation in a way where everyone can actually be heard?" or "Given how important this is, what kind of process would give everyone confidence we've thought through all perspectives?" or

"Would it be helpful to take a break, try a different approach, or change something about how we're doing this?" These interventions acknowledge that the process itself may need modification to support the outcomes everyone desires.

Cultural Considerations and Humility

The four-step model must be adapted thoughtfully across different cultural contexts while maintaining its core principles of dignity, respect, and empowerment. Cultural humility represents a paradigm shift from traditional concepts of cultural competence. While competence suggests mastery, humility acknowledges the impossibility of fully understanding another's cultural experience.

Core principles of cultural humility include recognizing our limitations in fully comprehending the depth of someone else's cultural reality, maintaining a learner's mindset where each cross-cultural interaction becomes an opportunity to learn, centering others' voices by prioritizing their perspectives rather than making assumptions, engaging in ongoing self-examination by continuously reflecting on how our cultural background influences our perceptions, and acknowledging power dynamics by recognizing how systemic inequalities shape current conflicts.

Cultural adaptations in practice require sensitivity to different communication styles. Some cultures value directness while others prefer indirect approaches that preserve harmony. You might need to adjust directness levels in acknowledgment statements, use more tentative language in cultures that value harmony, allow more processing time in cultures that emphasize reflection, and include family or community voices when culturally appropriate.

Authority relationships vary significantly across cultures, requiring modifications to empowerment approaches to respect cultural authority structures, inclusion of relevant cultural leaders in conflict resolution processes, adaptation of validation to honor cultural values about respect and hierarchy, and recognition that some cultures express care through action rather than words.

Emotional expression norms also differ across cultures. Some cultures value emotional restraint while others encourage more open expression. Effective practitioners respect cultures where emotional restraint is valued, understand that apparent lack of emotion doesn't indicate lack of caring, adapt validation approaches to cultural norms about emotional sharing, and recognize that some cultures express care through action rather than words.

Essential Skills for Sustained Connection

Learning to introduce difficult topics without triggering defensiveness requires careful attention to timing and approach.

You might say: "I'd like to talk about something that might be sensitive. How would that feel for you?" or "There's an issue I think we need to address. Are you in a space where you can engage with something potentially challenging?" This approach respects the other person's readiness and creates collaborative entry into difficult territory.

Maintaining necessary limits while preserving relationships requires clear communication about boundaries combined with genuine care. You might say: "I care about our relationship, and I also need to be clear about what I can and cannot do" or "I want to support you, and I also have some constraints I need to work within." This approach maintains connection while establishing realistic expectations.

Helping frame conversations in larger contexts of growth and understanding can transform how people experience conflict. You might observe: "This conversation feels difficult, and I think that's because it matters to both of us" or "Working through this conflict might actually strengthen our relationship in the long run." This reframing helps people see beyond immediate discomfort to longer-term benefits.

Measuring Success Differently

When applying these approaches effectively, success looks different than simply "problem solved." Relationship changes become evident through increased trust after working through conflict, improved team capacity for having difficult conversations, people's ability to disagree without damaging relationships, and groups becoming more creative and collaborative in their approach to challenges.

Learning and growth indicators include individuals developing better emotional intelligence and conflict skills, organizations improving at handling complexity and uncertainty, innovation emerging from productive disagreement, and culture shifting toward greater psychological safety where people feel secure expressing different viewpoints.

Systemic impact manifests through fewer conflicts escalating to formal processes, higher engagement and retention in organizations, better decision-making through inclusion of diverse voices, and more resilient and adaptable systems that can handle change and challenge more effectively.

These broader measures of success recognize that the four-step model's impact extends far beyond individual conversations to influence organizational culture, relationship quality, and collective capacity for navigating complexity.

Conclusion: The Art of Sustained Connection

The journey from initial connection to sustained dialogue through difficult conversations represents one of the most sophisticated forms of human interaction. It requires integration of neuroscience knowledge, practical skills, cultural humility, and genuine commitment to relationship. The Four-Step MindSet Model—Acknowledgment, Acceptance, Validation, and Empowerment—provides the foundational structure, but skilled dialogue goes beyond any single framework to become a way of being with others that honors both individual dignity and collective wisdom.

When we approach difficult dialogue with the skills and mindset outlined in this chapter, we don't just resolve immediate conflicts—we contribute to a cultural evolution toward more humane, effective ways of engaging with difference and disagreement. The stories we've explored—from Fredrick's academic struggles to complex team conflicts—demonstrate that these skills are not just theoretical ideals but practical tools that can transform real situations.

Each difficult conversation becomes an opportunity to practice presence, empathy, and curiosity. Each conflict becomes a chance to choose connection over control. The choice is always before us: Will we approach difficult conversations as battles to be won or as opportunities for mutual understanding? Will we use conflict to prove our point or to discover new possibilities? Will we choose the courage required for authentic dialogue or retreat to the safety of positions and defenses?

The path forward requires both skill and heart, both technique and genuine care for one another's wellbeing. In choosing this path, we become agents of transformation in a world that desperately needs more connection, understanding, and hope. The mastery of difficult conversations—whether one-on-one or in groups—creates the foundation for broader transformation. Yet the true test of these principles lies not in isolated interventions but in their systematic application within the institutions where we spend our lives.

The same neurobiological principles that guide individual crisis response can reshape educational cultures when applied with intentional consistency. The four-step model that works in moments of acute conflict can prevent countless crises when embedded in the daily rhythms of school life. Most importantly, the connection skills that heal relationships can become the foundation for environments where all students—regardless of their challenges or backgrounds—can experience what it means to be truly seen, understood, and valued.

Questions for Personal Reflection or Group Discussion

Consider these questions individually or discuss with colleagues to deepen your understanding of maintaining connection through complex and ongoing challenges.

Understanding the Four-Step Model

1. **Step-by-Step Reflection** Think through a recent difficult conversation using the four-step framework. At which step did you feel most confident? Which step was most challenging for you? How might better mastery of each step change your approach?
2. **Empowerment vs. Permissiveness** Reflect on the difference between empowering choice and avoiding necessary boundaries. How do you maintain appropriate limits while still honoring someone's autonomy and dignity?

Application to Your Practice

3. **Sustained Dialogue Skills** Consider an ongoing challenging relationship in your work. How could you apply the four-step model not just in crisis moments, but as a way of building and maintaining the relationship over time?

4. **Group Dynamics** Think about a time when you needed to facilitate dialogue among multiple people with different perspectives. How might the four-step model apply to group situations? What additional skills would you need to develop?

Systemic Reflection

5. **Organizational Dialogue Culture** How does your organization handle ongoing conflicts or disagreements? What would it look like to embed the four-step model into regular team meetings, policy discussions, or conflict resolution procedures?

Integration Practice: Choose one ongoing challenging relationship and intentionally apply the four-step model in your next three interactions. Document what you notice about changes in the relationship dynamic.

References

Coleman, P. T., Deutsch, M., & Marcus, E. C. (Eds.). (2014). *The handbook of conflict resolution: Theory and practice* (3rd ed.). Jossey-Bass.

Deci, E. L., & Ryan, R. M. (2000). The "what" and "why" of goal pursuits: Human needs and the self-determination of behavior. *Psychological Inquiry*, 11(4), 227-268.

Fisher, R., Ury, W., & Patton, B. (2011). *Getting to yes: Negotiating agreement without giving in* (3rd ed.). Penguin Books.

Gottman, J., & Silver, N. (2015). *The seven principles for making marriage work* (Rev. ed.). Harmony Books.

Lieberman, M. D., Eisenberger, N. I., Crockett, M. J., Tom, S. M., Pfeifer, J. H., & Way, B. M. (2007). Putting feelings into words: Affect labeling disrupts amygdala activity in response to affective stimuli. *Psychological Science*, 18(5), 421-428.

Patterson, K., Grenny, J., McMillan, R., & Switzler, A. (2011). *Crucial conversations: Tools for talking when stakes are high* (2nd ed.). McGraw-Hill Education.

Siegel, D. J. (2012). *The developing mind: How relationships and the brain interact to shape who we are* (2nd ed.). Guilford Press.

Stone, D., Patton, B., & Heen, S. (2010). *Difficult conversations: How to discuss what matters most* (Rev. ed.). Penguin Books.

Walton, G. M., & Cohen, G. L. (2007). A question of belonging: Race, social fit, and achievement. *Journal of Personality and Social Psychology*, 93(1), 82-96.

Chapter 7: The Power of Intentional Connection - Building a Culture of Prevention in Educational Settings

In educational settings across the world, a quiet revolution is taking place. Educators are discovering that brief moments of connection between teachers and students serve as critical intervention points that can prevent crises before they begin. These "micro-moments" of attunement—the ability to perceive and respond to another person's internal state—represent opportunities for what Dr. Daniel Siegel calls neural integration: the linking of differentiated parts of the nervous system that creates coherence, adaptability, and well-being.

From an Interpersonal Neurobiology (IPNB) perspective, these moments literally shape the architecture of students' developing brains through relational experiences between minds (Siegel, 2012). When educators develop the ability to recognize subtle shifts in students' emotional states, they can respond with intentional connection before minor struggles escalate into full-blown crises.

This chapter explores how understanding the neuroscience of connection transforms educational practice, moving from reactive crisis management to proactive relationship-building that creates the conditions in which all students can thrive.

The Neuroscience of Connection: Why Relationships Matter for Learning

Dr. Stephen Porges's Polyvagal Theory explains how our nervous system constantly scans for cues of safety or threat—a process called neuroception (Porges, 2011). This evolutionary mechanism triggers states of either defense or connection without conscious thought. Understanding this biological reality transforms how we approach student behavior and learning.

Positive social interactions, marked by warm expressions, soothing tones, and open body language, activate our social engagement system and create the foundation for all learning and growth. Recent brain imaging studies show that supportive interactions decrease activity in threat-detection circuits while increasing activity in networks related to reward, empathy, and self-regulation.

When students perceive safety in your presence—through your calm voice, open posture, and genuine attention—their brains shift from defensive mode to learning mode. Your regulated state becomes a "neural signal" that dysregulated students can connect to. This means that your internal state directly impacts student learning capacity.

If you approach a struggling student while feeling frustrated or rushed, your nervous system signals threat, potentially escalating their distress. Conversely, when you pause to center yourself—taking three deep breaths, relaxing your shoulders, and genuinely focusing on understanding rather than controlling—you create an invisible field of safety that students can feel.

Before approaching a dysregulated student, do a quick internal check: "What is my nervous system doing right now?" If you notice tension, urgency, or frustration, take time to regulate yourself first. Students will unconsciously mirror your state, so your calm presence becomes your most powerful intervention tool.

Recognizing Early Warning Signs: The Power of Prevention

Behavioral escalation rarely occurs without warning. Educators who are trained to notice early signals can intervene at the pivotal moment—the point where a small, well-timed intervention can prevent a major behavioral crisis. Key indicators that often precede escalation include changes in vocal tone and volume, increased motor activity, shifts in facial coloration, altered breathing patterns, and subtle changes in facial expressions.

By recognizing these signals, educators can offer support precisely when students are most receptive—when their nervous systems are still within the "window of tolerance," the optimal zone of arousal for learning and connection.

During transitions or challenging activities, scan the room for these early warning signs. Practice neutral observation by saying, "I notice your shoulders look tense," rather than, "You need to calm down." Neutral observation reduces defensiveness by simply reflecting what you see rather than telling someone what to do or how to feel.

It builds self-awareness by pointing out physical cues in a nonjudgmental way, helping children develop awareness of their internal states. Over time, they'll start noticing these signs themselves. This approach also maintains connection by keeping you in a supportive role rather than an adversarial one, working together to understand what's happening instead of trying to control behavior.

Examples of neutral observation during transitions include:

- "I see you're moving more slowly today."
- "Your voice sounds different right now."
- "I notice you keep looking at the door."
- "Your hands are making fists."

The key is staying curious rather than corrective. When children feel understood rather than managed, they are much more likely to accept support and develop their own coping strategies. This approach also helps you catch escalation early, when intervention is most effective and gentle.

Relationships as the Foundation for Learning

Research demonstrates that supportive relationships are the primary mechanism through which children develop the skills necessary for success. Studies identify relationships as the "active ingredient" in effective educational practices—the crucial element that activates and amplifies all other interventions.

Educational neuroscientist Mary Helen Immordino-Yang's research shows that emotional engagement is essential for deep learning. We cannot think deeply about things that do not connect to our emotional selves. Meaningful learning occurs within the context of relationships that matter to us (Immordino-Yang, 2016). This understanding helps explain why instructional interventions often fail with students experiencing behavioral challenges. Without a relational foundation, even well-researched strategies may fall short.

Every interaction with a caring adult presents what researchers call contingent communication—responsive, timely interactions in which the educator perceives the student's internal state and responds in a way that promotes the developing capacity for self-regulation. This process literally sculpts neural pathways through repeated experiences of "feeling felt."

The MindSet Four-Step Model in Educational Practice

Building on the four-step framework introduced in Chapter 6, we now explore how Acknowledgment, Acceptance, Validation, and Empowerment take on particular significance in educational settings. These elements directly impact learning capacity, classroom climate, and long-term student development.

Understanding how to adapt these four steps for the unique dynamics of schools requires attention to students' developmental needs, the constraints of educational environments, and the many relationships that shape student experiences.

From Clinical to Educational: Key Adaptations

While the core principles remain constant, applying the four-step model in educational settings requires specific adjustments. Students at different ages need varying levels of scaffolding for emotional awareness and decision-making.

Elementary students benefit from simple, concrete language, while high school students can engage with more complex emotional vocabulary. The presence of peers adds complexity to the validation and empowerment steps. Additionally, school policies and time limitations require creative adaptations. Educational settings also offer unique opportunities for proactive relationship-building, rather than relying solely on crisis response.

Elementary Example: Marcus and the Math Meltdown

Eight-year-old Marcus throws his pencil across the room during a math lesson, shouting, "I hate this stupid work!"

> **Acknowledgment (Adapted for Age):** "Marcus, I see you threw your pencil, and I heard you say you're upset about the math work." (Simple, concrete observation)

Acceptance (Developmentally Appropriate): "It looks like the math is feeling really hard right now."(Connecting behavior to feeling using age-appropriate language)

Validation (Child-Friendly): "Math can be really frustrating sometimes. It makes sense that you'd feel upset when something is hard." (Normalizing the struggle without complex explanations)

Empowerment (Scaffolded Choices): "What would help you with the math right now? Would you like to take a break, work with a partner, or try a different problem first?" (Limited, concrete options appropriate for his developmental level)

Middle School Example: Sarah's Social Media Crisis

Thirteen-year-old Sarah is discovered crying in the bathroom after seeing hurtful posts about her on social media.

Acknowledgment: "Sarah, I can see you're really upset, and I noticed you're here by yourself during lunch."

Acceptance: "It seems like something happened that hurt your feelings pretty deeply."

Validation: "Middle school social situations can be incredibly painful. When people say hurtful things, especially online where others can see it, that would be devastating for anyone."

Empowerment: "You've dealt with difficult social situations before. What feels like the most important thing to address first? Do you want to talk about how to handle the online situation, or would it help to identify some supportive friends you could connect with?"

High School Example: Building on Success

Following successful crisis interventions using the four-step model, educators can build more supportive classroom systems by incorporating these steps proactively:

Proactive Acknowledgment: Teachers begin checking in with students showing early signs of stress.

Example: "I notice you seem worried about the upcoming deadline."

Systemic Acceptance: Classroom norms acknowledge emotional realities.

Example: "Big projects can bring up lots of feelings—stress, excitement, worry. That's all normal."

Cultural Validation: Educators validate diverse student experiences.

Example: "Everyone's home life looks different, and that affects how you approach schoolwork. Your circumstances don't determine your worth."

Structural Empowerment: Choice is built into classroom systems.

Example: "Projects can be completed in multiple formats. What approach would help you show your learning best?"

Adapting for Diverse Educational Needs

Students with Disabilities

Adaptations for acknowledgment include using visual supports for students with processing differences, offering multiple ways to communicate observations (such as verbal, written, or pictorial formats), and accounting for sensory sensitivities in how acknowledgment is delivered.

Example: For a student with autism experiencing sensory overload:"I notice the lights seem very bright right now, and you've moved to the corner of the room."

English Language Learners

Adaptations for acceptance involve using simpler language structures for identifying emotions, providing emotion cards or visual supports, and allowing extra processing time for emotional vocabulary.

Example:

"You look... worried? Sad? Help me understand."

(This offers specific emotion words with a questioning tone to invite clarification.)

Culturally Diverse Students

Validation adaptations require recognizing cultural differences in emotional expression, understanding the family and community contexts that influence behavior, and avoiding assumptions about what is considered an "appropriate" emotional response.

Example: For a student from a culture that values family obligation:

"Taking care of family is really important to you. It makes sense that you'd feel torn between family responsibilities and school demands."

Creating Classroom Cultures of Connection

The foundation of any relationship-centered classroom begins with intentional attention to both the physical environment students inhabit and the social atmosphere they experience from the moment they enter. Creating environments that support nervous system regulation is essential, as students learn best when they feel genuinely safe—physically and emotionally.

The physical environment profoundly impacts student well-being in ways educators are only beginning to fully understand. Natural lighting, when available, helps reduce stress hormones and supports healthy circadian rhythms, which influence attention span and emotional regulation. Controlled noise levels prevent sensory overload that can trigger fight-or-flight responses, especially in students who have experienced trauma or who have heightened sensitivities. Maintaining comfortable temperatures supports physiological regulation, and minimizing visual clutter helps reduce cognitive load so students can focus their energy on learning rather than managing environmental distractions.

Just as important are clear sight lines and accessible exit routes, which provide a sense of psychological safety even at a subconscious level. Students need to feel they have options and are not trapped—even when they consciously know they are safe. Flexible seating options acknowledge that different nervous systems have different needs. Some students focus better while moving, others need the security of a defined personal space, and some benefit from varied textures or seating positions for sensory input.

Routine and predictability act as neurological anchors in the often chaotic lives of students. Consistent daily schedules offer the safety of knowing what to expect, allowing students to lower their guard and engage more fully in learning. When changes are necessary, transparent communication helps reduce anxiety and supports students' sense of control and agency. Clear expectations and procedures reduce the cognitive effort required for navigating social norms, freeing up mental resources for academic engagement.

Multiple planned connection points throughout the day build what can be described as "relationship capital"—the trust and goodwill that make meaningful learning possible. These moments are not elaborate interventions but simple, consistent gestures of human recognition woven into daily instruction.

The social environment includes the countless daily interactions that either build or erode a student's sense of belonging and self-worth. Personal greetings provide individual acknowledgment that lets each student know their presence matters. Brief check-ins during work time maintain connection without disrupting the learning process, allowing educators to monitor both academic progress and emotional well-being in real time.

Recognition of effort and growth, rather than just achievement, reinforces the intrinsic motivation that leads to sustained learning. When students know their struggles and progress are seen and valued, they're more likely to persist through difficulties and take the risks necessary for growth. Peer support systems multiply connection opportunities beyond what any single teacher could provide, creating networks of care that extend throughout the classroom community.

Perhaps most powerfully, conflict resolution processes that model healthy relationship skills teach students invaluable life capabilities while strengthening rather than damaging classroom relationships. When conflicts become opportunities for learning and growth rather than simply problems to be managed, students develop the emotional intelligence and interpersonal skills they'll need throughout their lives.

Understanding Student Needs Through a Relational Lens

Research by Mitch Weathers introduces the concept of "Chaos Navigators"—students who spend much of their energy just surviving the unpredictability of their lives outside school. These young people arrive each day having already used significant cognitive resources to manage their complex realities.

When classrooms provide reliable structure and neurobiologically supportive environments, something transformational happens. Students can begin to redirect their attention and energy away from vigilance and survival. Instead of scanning for threats or navigating sensory overwhelm, they are freed to engage with learning, build relationships, and explore their potential.

Weaving Connection Into Daily Practice

The beauty of relationship-centered teaching lies not in grand gestures, but in the countless small moments that make up a school day. Morning connections offer natural opportunities to apply relational principles through simple check-ins that acknowledge students' reality. For example:

"I notice some of you look tired this morning. Starting the day can be hard sometimes. What would help you feel ready to learn?"

Transitions present another powerful opportunity for connection. Rather than rushing students from one activity to another, skilled educators use acknowledgment during difficult moments: "I see several people looking worried about the test. Test anxiety is really common and makes sense." This validation doesn't eliminate the challenge, but it normalizes the struggle and creates space for students to process their emotions rather than becoming overwhelmed by them.

Conflict prevention becomes possible when educators attune to early warning signs before situations escalate. A teacher might notice tension building during group work and address it directly: "I notice some tension in the group work. What's happening that we should talk about?" This proactive approach prevents small frustrations from becoming major disruptions while teaching students to recognize and address interpersonal challenges constructively.

Building Educator Capacity for Relational Teaching

Sustainable implementation of relationship-centered practices requires more than surface-level strategies. Educators need a deep understanding of how the four-step model—Acknowledgment, Acceptance, Validation, and Empowerment—adapts across developmental stages.

Elementary students benefit from simple, concrete language that aligns with their cognitive development. High school students, by contrast, are often ready to engage with more complex emotional vocabulary and nuanced relationship dynamics.

Cultural responsiveness demands that educators understand how the four-step model adapts for diverse student populations while maintaining its core integrity. This means recognizing how different cultures express distress, seek help, and respond to authority figures. A student from a culture that values indirect communication may signal distress very differently than one from a more direct cultural background, yet both deserve the same quality of connection and support.

Perhaps most critically, educators must build their own self-regulation skills in order to maintain the calm, grounded presence needed for co-regulation with students. This includes reflecting honestly on personal triggers, developing effective self-regulation strategies, and understanding how educator stress impacts classroom dynamics. When teachers are overwhelmed or dysregulated, students sense that energy, which can make learning more difficult for everyone.

Creating Collaborative Learning Communities

One-time training events, while often well-meaning, rarely create lasting changes in educational practice. Lasting impact comes from collaborative professional learning communities where educators engage in ongoing reflection and shared practice.

In these communities, teachers practice the four-step model with feedback from colleagues, examining real student scenarios through the relational framework rather than simply discussing theory.

These learning communities become safe spaces where educators share both successes and challenges in implementation, supporting each other through the inevitable difficulties of changing established practices. Most importantly, they help educators develop the personal regulation skills necessary for effective relationship-building while creating shared language and approaches that strengthen school-wide culture.

Administrative Leadership for a Relational Culture

School policies must actively support relationship-building approaches rather than inadvertently undermining them. Discipline policies that focus on learning rather than punishment, include restorative elements, and consider contextual factors in behavioral responses send clear messages about school values. Time protection becomes essential as administrators recognize that meaningful relationship-building requires unhurried interactions, not rushed exchanges between classes.

Resource allocation reflects priorities, and schools committed to relational approaches provide the materials, spaces, and staffing necessary to support both environmental and programmatic needs. This could include creating quiet areas for difficult conversations, scheduling professional development on relational skills, or maintaining class sizes that allow for individualized attention.

Above all, administrators must model the same connection principles they expect teachers to use with students. This means using the four-step model when interacting with staff, acknowledging the challenges of teaching, validating educators' concerns, and empowering them with meaningful choices in their professional roles. When teachers experience this kind of support from leadership, they are far more likely to extend it to their students.

The Expanding Impact of Relational Investment

The effects of relationship-centered education extend far beyond individual classrooms, creating positive ripple effects throughout the entire school community. Students who feel genuinely connected demonstrate increased academic engagement through greater participation, sustained effort, and willingness to take the intellectual risks necessary for deep learning. Roorda and colleagues' comprehensive meta-analysis of 99 studies involving over 160,000 students found medium to large positive associations between positive teacher-student relationships and both engagement and achievement.

Social emotional development flourishes as students develop improved self-regulation, empathy, and conflict resolution skills. They begin applying similar relational approaches with their peers, creating more supportive classroom cultures. Behavioral indicators shift dramatically with decreased office referrals, increased help-seeking behaviors, and improved peer relationships as students feel safer and more supported in their learning environment.

The classroom climate transforms into one of psychological safety where students feel secure enough to make mistakes, ask questions, and take the academic risks necessary for genuine learning. Peer relationships improve as students begin using similar approaches with each other, and the entire learning culture shifts from compliance-based to curiosity-driven as students feel safe to engage authentically with challenging material.

Educator Transformation and Satisfaction

Teachers report profound changes in their professional experience when equipped with effective relationship-building skills. Job satisfaction increases as educators feel more capable of connecting meaningfully with students, even those who present significant challenges. As teachers gain confidence in handling difficult situations, their sense of professional efficacy also grows, leading to a stronger belief in their own competence and effectiveness.

This individual transformation contributes to a broader collaborative culture. Educators who experience supportive relationships with leadership are more likely to collaborate effectively with colleagues. Over time, the positive culture becomes self-reinforcing: success leads to more success, and educators feel increasingly capable and supported in their essential work.

Measuring Meaningful Change

While quantitative data provides important baseline information, the most compelling evidence of relational transformation often appears in the qualitative changes that shape school culture. Academic indicators—such as grade point averages, assignment completion rates, and attendance—tell part of the story. Behavioral data, including office referrals, suspension rates, and reports of peer conflict, also offer valuable insights.

However, the deeper impact emerges through student voice in focus groups about school experience, stories of meaningful teacher connections, and descriptions of how conflicts are resolved constructively. Educator reflection captures changes in approach to challenging behaviors, growing confidence in relationship-building skills, and powerful stories of successful connections with previously difficult students.

Family feedback offers another crucial perspective. Parents frequently report improved communication with teachers, noticeable changes in their child's attitude toward school, and growing trust in the school's ability to support their child's overall development. These qualitative insights often reveal the most significant and lasting impacts of relationship-centered approaches.

Overcoming Implementation Challenges

Time constraints remain one of the most common barriers to implementing relationship-centered practices. Teachers often feel overwhelmed by academic demands and perceive a lack of time for connection. The solution lies not in adding more activities but in weaving connection strategies into existing routines. Morning greetings, conversations during transitions, and feedback moments all offer natural, time-efficient opportunities to apply the four-step model.

Skeptical staff members may view relationship approaches as ineffective or worry about losing classroom authority. Research consistently demonstrates that connection actually enhances rather than undermines effective classroom management by building the trust and respect necessary for student cooperation. Clear examples of how the model maintains appropriate boundaries while strengthening relationships help address these concerns.

Large class sizes and diverse student populations can make individualized connection feel overwhelming, but educators can learn to recognize patterns across groups while maintaining individual responsiveness. Peer support systems and classroom structures that facilitate multiple connection points help extend the teacher's capacity for relationship-building beyond what any individual could accomplish alone.

Systemic barriers require more comprehensive solutions through policy alignment with relationship-centered values and stakeholder engagement in understanding the research foundation for connection-focused approaches. When entire school systems embrace relational principles, individual educators find their efforts supported rather than undermined by broader institutional culture.

Conclusion: From Individual Connection to Educational Transformation

The journey toward intentional connection in education reveals a powerful truth: the same neurobiological principles that heal individual relationships can transform entire learning communities. When we understand that behavior is communication, that safety is a prerequisite for learning, and that connection is a pathway to healing, we create environments where all students can thrive.

The research is both clear and consistent. Roorda's meta-analysis shows a strong connection between positive teacher-student relationships and academic engagement and achievement. Emerging classroom neuroscience reveals brain-to-brain synchrony between regulated educators and their students. This body of evidence supports what many educators have long sensed: relationships are not just helpful in the learning process—they are the foundation of it.

The MindSet Four-Step Model—Acknowledgment, Acceptance, Validation, and Empowerment—offers more than a crisis-response framework. When adapted for daily educational practice, it becomes a tool for transformation. It honors the dignity and agency of each student while creating the neurobiological conditions necessary for learning and growth.

When educators master the skills of neutral observation, learn to recognize and validate emotional states, and consistently offer empowering choices, they become more than instructors. They become catalysts for healing, growth, and lifelong change in the lives of their students.

Questions for Personal Reflection or Group Discussion

Consider these questions individually or discuss them with colleagues to deepen your understanding of how intentional connection can prevent crises and strengthen learning communities.

Understanding Prevention Through Connection

1. **Early Warning Recognition** Reflect on your ability to notice early signs of dysregulation in students or colleagues. What subtle cues do you typically pick up on? How could increasing your awareness of these early signals help you intervene more effectively before a situation escalates?
2. **Your Nervous System as a Tool** Think about how your own nervous system state influences the learning environment. What strategies help you stay calm and present enough to support others through co-regulation? How do you become aware when your stress level begins to affect those around you?

Application to Your Practice

3. **Environmental Assessment** Evaluate your classroom or work environment through the lens of nervous system regulation. Which elements support a sense of calm and connection? What small changes could you make to create a space that is more supportive of regulation and learning?
4. **Relationship Investment** Consider students or colleagues who present the greatest relational challenges. How might investing in small, consistent moments of connection throughout the day shift those dynamics? What specific actions—however small—could you take to build relationship capital with them?

Systemic Reflection

5. **Culture of Prevention** Examine how your school or organization currently balances relationship-building with crisis response. To move toward a true culture of prevention through connection, what systems, mindsets, or policies would need to change?

Integration Practice

This week, identify one person who shows early signs of stress or dysregulation. Intentionally offer brief moments of connection before a crisis can develop. Observe how these preventive interactions influence your ongoing relationship and the broader learning environment.

References

Durlak, J. A., Weissberg, R. P., Dymnicki, A. B., Taylor, R. D., & Schellinger, K. B. (2011). The impact of enhancing students' social and emotional learning: A meta-analysis of school-based universal interventions. *Child Development*, 82(1), 405-432. https://doi.org/10.1111/j.1467-8624.2010.01564.x

Immordino-Yang, M. H. (2016). *Emotions, learning, and the brain: Exploring the educational implications of affective neuroscience*. W. W. Norton & Company.

Porges, S. W. (2011). *The polyvagal theory: Neurophysiological foundations of emotions, attachment, communication, and self-regulation*. W. W. Norton & Company.

Roorda, D. L., Koomen, H. M. Y., Spilt, J. L., & Oort, F. J. (2011). The influence of affective teacher-student relationships on students' school engagement and achievement: A meta-analytic approach. *Review of Educational Research*, 81(4), 493-529. https://doi.org/10.3102/0034654311421793

Siegel, D. J. (2012). *The developing mind: How relationships and the brain interact to shape who we are* (2nd ed.). Guilford Press.

Weathers, M. (2023). Executive functions for every classroom: Creating predictable learning environments. Corwin

Chapter 8: From Leadership to Legacy - Transforming Organizational Culture Through Conflict

A Principal's Dawn Reflection

In the quiet moments before dawn, school principal Elena Martinez sits at her desk, reviewing notes from yesterday's heated faculty meeting. The tension between traditional and progressive discipline approaches had sparked passionate debates, threatening to divide her staff. Rather than immediately imposing a solution, Elena recognized the situation as an opportunity to demonstrate transformative leadership in action.

Her insight reflects a fundamental truth: effective leadership in conflict resolution isn't about wielding authority. It's about creating spaces where diverse perspectives can coexist and where conflict becomes a catalyst for growth. This chapter explores how the four-step model can scale beyond individual interactions to reshape entire organizational cultures, using Elena's journey as a practical guide.

The Architecture of Conflict-Positive Organizations

Traditional organizational structures often treat conflict as a system failure—something to minimize, contain, or resolve quickly. In contrast, conflict-positive organizations recognize that productive conflict is essential infrastructure for adaptation, innovation, and authentic relationship-building.

Elena discovered this when she realized that her faculty's disciplinary debate reflected deeper tensions related to educational identity, generational differences, and shifting student needs. Rather than viewing the situation as a problem to solve, she began to see it as valuable organizational intelligence.

Understanding Conflict as Information

In conflict-positive organizations, disagreement serves multiple functions:

- It acts as a catalyst for innovation. Diverse perspectives in productive tension generate more creative solutions than homogeneous agreement.Conflict functions as an early warning system, signaling underlying systemic issues before they become crises. Successfully navigated conflicts build stronger, more resilient working relationships through relationship strengthening. Organizations engaging conflict well develop greater adaptive capacity to navigate change. Working through conflicts clarifies and strengthens shared values through cultural alignment.

Cultural Wisdom in Conflict Transformation

While the MindSet Safety Management approach is grounded in universal principles of safety and dignity, it must also adapt to diverse cultural frameworks. Key variations include:

- Communication styles: Direct versus indirect approaches to preserve dignity.
- Community focus: Balancing individual accountability with family or community involvement.
- Emotional expression: Controlled versus passionate engagement as a sign of care.
- Time orientation: Weighing efficiency against relationship maintenance.
- Authority dynamics: Differing expectations around hierarchical engagement.

Elena learned to ask about communication preferences, involve relevant family or community members when appropriate, and honor cultural strengths while upholding core safety principles. The key is cultural humility—recognizing that our approaches are culturally specific and remaining curious about each person's framework without stereotyping.

Designing for Productive Tension

Research by Amy Edmondson reveals that high-performing teams experience more conflict than low-performing ones—but they've learned to engage constructively. Elena implemented conflict-positive organizational design through several elements including structured dissent protocols, conflict competence development, and psychological safety infrastructure.

Elena created "perspective circles" where participants explored issues from multiple viewpoints before attempting consensus. The process included issue presentation with clear description of the challenge, perspective taking by exploring the issue from different stakeholder viewpoints, assumption surfacing to identify underlying beliefs driving positions, creative integration through collaborative solution generation honoring multiple perspectives, and decision process with clear criteria for moving from exploration to decision.

ElenaShe also arranged professional development sessions focused on understanding stress responses, recognizing escalation patterns, and practicing integrative thinking. Core competencies included self-awareness, emotional regulation, perspective-taking, and communication skills.

Elena fostered an environment where it was safe to disagree, challenge authority, and admit mistakes. She modeled values consistently, made decisions transparently, and practiced appropriate vulnerability as a leader.

The Three Pillars of Leadership Implementation

Elena's approach rested on three interconnected foundations: emotional **intelligence**, authentic **presence**, and systematic **understanding**. Her leadership consistently embodied the four-step principles—Acknowledgment, Acceptance, Validation, and Empowerment—scaled across systems.

Key Organizational Transformation Factors

Elena's success came from systematically addressing multiple organizational elements.

Leadership Prerequisites:

- Emotional intelligence in conflict situations
- Authentic presence during difficult conversations
- Systematic understanding of neurobiological principles

- Consistent modeling of four-step principles

Cultural Infrastructure:

- Structured processes for productive disagreement
- Conflict competence development for all staff
- Psychological safety as an organizational foundation
- Clear non-negotiables with flexibility in implementation

Sustainability Elements:

- Embedded professional learning communities
- Distributed leadership development
- Regular assessment of transformation progress
- Integration of conflict-positive practices into daily operations

Pillar 1: Emotional Intelligence in Conflict Leadership

When Elena became aware of faculty tension, her first step wasn't to solve the problem. Instead, she focused on deeply understanding it. Through one-on-one conversations, she discovered that traditional teachers felt their experience was being devalued, while progressive faculty feared falling behind emerging trends.

Elena's insight revealed that the conflict wasn't just about disciplinary methods—it was rooted in identity, professional validation, and fear of change. Her organizational-level application of the four-step model began with acknowledgment. She observed that faculty were experiencing philosophical tension around discipline and that passionate educators on different sides of the issue were struggling to collaborate effectively.

Institutional acceptance recognized that this debate brought up deeper concerns about educational identity and professional validation—significant emotional territories for educators who care deeply. Cultural validation emphasized that this debate showed faculty strength, with tensions existing because they had both experienced educators and innovative thinkers committed to student success.

Organizational empowerment asked what process would help integrate wisdom from different approaches and how they might create space for both proven methods and innovative strategies.

Building Organizational Capacity for Transformation

Developing Shared Language and Frameworks

Elena focused on helping faculty master the four-step model at both individual and group levels. This work created a common vocabulary and shared frameworks for addressing conflict constructively.

Creating Support Structures

She established both formal and informal structures to support collaborative problem-solving. These included:

- Regular meetings with dedicated time for conflict resolution
- Cross-perspective mentoring, pairing traditional and progressive faculty
- Professional learning communities exploring a range of disciplinary frameworks
- Clear protocols, including formal conflict resolution pathways and mediation resources

Empowering Distributed Leadership

Elena cultivated leadership throughout the staff by identifying informal leaders, offering development opportunities, establishing working groups, and encouraging peer coaching relationships.

Balancing Accountability and Support

Elena articulated clear, non-negotiable values while allowing implementation flexibility. Core non-negotiables included student dignity in all disciplinary approaches, learning-focused consequences promoting growth, equity considerations addressing cultural and historical contexts, and restorative elements repairing harm and rebuilding relationships.

She provided differentiated support through individual coaching, peer observation, reflection protocols, and adequate resources matched to expectations.

Creating a Culture of Constructive Conflict

Elena worked systematically to build an environment where differences were expected, respected, and used as a source of organizational learning.

Normalizing Productive Disagreement

Elena reframed conflict as learning opportunity through modeling curiosity, creating language for productive conflict, and celebrating constructive disagreement when it led to creative solutions.

Building Integrative Thinking Capacity

Elena expanded staff capacity for holding opposing ideas in tension and generating solutions honoring multiple insights. She taught both-and mindset, polarity thinking, and facilitated processes creating synthetic solutions through appreciative inquiry and collaborative prototyping.

Conflict as Innovation Catalyst

Elena learned to maintain creative tension through divergent-convergent rhythms, enhanced devil's advocacy, and scenario planning. She orchestrated conflicts between different constituencies productively using systems thinking and cross-functional integration strategies.

The Faculty Meeting Crisis: Elena's Four-Step Model in Action

To illustrate how these principles work in practice, we return to the heated faculty meeting that opened this chapter, where Elena applied the four-step model to navigate organizational conflict.

The tension in the room was palpable when veteran teacher Mrs. Hawkins raised her voice.

"These new approaches are just permissive nonsense! When I started teaching twenty years ago, we had respect in classrooms because students knew there were real consequences for their actions. Now we're supposed to validate every feeling and ask permission before enforcing basic rules?"

Newer teacher Ms. Rodriguez responded with equal intensity.

"But we know better now! The research is clear that punitive approaches harm students, especially those who've experienced trauma. We can't keep perpetuating systems that hurt kids just because that's how we've always done things!"

The room visibly divided—older teachers nodding with Mrs. Hawkins, younger faculty aligning with Ms. Rodriguez. Side conversations erupted. Body language became closed and defensive. Elena could see her staff polarizing right in front of her.

Elena's Organizational Acknowledgment

Rather than calling for order or taking sides, Elena began with acknowledgment—the first step of the model—applied at the organizational level. She stood slowly, calm and composed, and spoke with genuine observation.

"I'm noticing some really passionate energy in this room right now. Mrs. Hawkins, I hear the intensity in your voice when you talk about respect and consequences. Ms. Rodriguez, I see how much you care about student wellbeing and trauma-responsive approaches. I'm observing that we have deeply committed educators on different sides of this conversation, and I can see how much this matters to everyone here."

Her acknowledgment didn't minimize the conflict or demand immediate calm. Instead, it created space for everyone to recognize the reality of what was happening—without judgment, blame, or premature resolution.

Organizational Acceptance

Moving to the second step, Elena addressed the emotional drivers beneath the surface disagreement.

"This conversation is bringing up some deep feelings for all of us. For those with years of experience, it might feel like your expertise and wisdom are being dismissed or devalued. For those newer to the profession, it might feel urgent to implement what you've learned about best practices, and frustrating when that feels blocked by tradition."

She paused, scanning the room with genuine care.

"These are significant emotional territories for educators who care deeply about students. This isn't just about discipline policies. This is about professional identity, about what it means to be effective teachers, about how we balance innovation with wisdom."

The room's energy shifted slightly as people felt seen in their deeper concerns, rather than just their stated positions.

Cultural Validation

Elena moved to validation, honoring both perspectives without taking sides.

"What I see in this room is actually our strength as a faculty. We have educators with decades of experience who have weathered multiple educational trends and know what actually works in classrooms over time. We also have educators bringing fresh perspectives and current research that challenges us to keep growing and improving."

She continued, "Mrs. Hawkins, your commitment to structure and accountability has helped countless students learn self-discipline and respect. Ms. Rodriguez, your focus on trauma-responsive practices addresses real needs we're seeing in our student population. Both of these perspectives are valuable, and the tension between them is actually productive. It means we care deeply about getting this right."

Organizational Empowerment

Finally, Elena moved to empowerment by involving the faculty in creating solutions instead of imposing them.

"So here's my question for all of us: How might we integrate the wisdom from both approaches? What would it look like to maintain high expectations and clear boundaries while also being responsive to trauma and individual student needs? Rather than choosing between these approaches, how might we create something that honors what's valuable in each?"

She proposed a process.

"I'd like to suggest we form working groups that include both experienced and newer teachers. Each group takes on a different aspect of our discipline approach—classroom management, consequences, family communication, crisis response. Spend the next month observing, researching, and designing approaches that integrate multiple perspectives."

"But here's the key. The solutions you develop need to address the concerns raised by both sides. They need to maintain the accountability and respect that Mrs. Hawkins values while incorporating the trauma-responsive, student-centered approaches that Ms. Rodriguez advocates."

The Ripple Effects: Six Months Later

The true test of Elena's approach didn't come during that single meeting but in how it transformed the school's culture over time. Six months later, the changes were visible throughout the building.

Collaborative Innovation

The working groups had developed discipline strategies that surprised everyone with their creativity. Instead of choosing between consequences and understanding, they created restorative practices that held students accountable while addressing underlying needs. Instead of rigid rules or permissive flexibility, they designed responsive structures that maintained high expectations and adapted to individual circumstances.

Mrs. Hawkins found herself mentoring Ms. Rodriguez in classroom management techniques that emphasized clear boundaries and mutual respect. Ms. Rodriguez shared research with Mrs. Hawkins about brain development and trauma responses, helping her understand why some traditional approaches hadn't worked with certain students.

Cultural Shift

The faculty had developed a new common language for discussing differences. When disagreements arose, staff naturally applied the four-step model. They acknowledged differing perspectives, accepted the emotional significance behind decisions, validated one another's concerns, and empowered each other to find shared solutions.

Teachers reported feeling safer expressing dissenting opinions during meetings. Innovation increased as a range of perspectives was welcomed instead of silenced. Student outcomes improved as the adults in the building modeled healthy conflict resolution.

Sustainable Leadership

Perhaps most importantly, Elena had fostered distributed leadership rather than creating dependency on her own conflict-resolution skills. When she was absent, faculty members facilitated difficult conversations using the same principles. When new conflicts emerged, staff had the tools to address them productively instead of avoiding or escalating them.

The school's culture had shifted from being conflict-avoidant to conflict-positive, from position-based argument to interest-based collaboration, and from win-lose dynamics to creative integration.

Challenges and Solutions in Organizational Transformation

Common Implementation Obstacles

Resistance to Change: Some staff members remained skeptical of conflict-positive approaches, viewing them as inefficient or unnecessarily complex.

Elena's Solution: She didn't try to convince resisters through argument. Instead, she created opportunities for them to experience the effectiveness of these approaches firsthand. She paired skeptical teachers with enthusiastic early adopters for specific projects, allowing natural mentoring and demonstration to occur.

Time Constraints: Faculty often felt too busy to invest in relationship-building and conflict resolution processes.

Elena's Solution: She demonstrated how these approaches actually saved time by preventing escalation and fostering more effective solutions. She integrated conflict competence development into existing professional development sessions rather than adding new requirements.

Hierarchy Challenges: Some staff members struggled with the collaborative nature of conflict resolution, preferring clear top-down directives.

Elena's Solution: She maintained clear decision-making authority while expanding the input and collaboration process. Staff understood that Elena would make final decisions when necessary, but those decisions would be informed by genuine engagement with multiple perspectives.

Sustainability Strategies

Elena embedded these practices into organizational DNA through policy integration, hiring practices that valued conflict competence, promotion criteria that included collaborative leadership skills, and ongoing professional development focused on relationship and communication skills.

The Leadership Legacy of Transformation

Elena's evolution—from managing faculty division to cultivating a conflict-positive organization—illustrates a shift from reactive crisis management to intentional cultural transformation. The principles of neurobiological awareness, empathic connection, skilled dialogue, and relationship-building scaled to create a learning organization capable of continuous adaptation through productive engagement with differences.

Organizations that foster cultures of productive disagreement outperform those that suppress conflict in innovation, adaptability, and sustainability. Elena's school saw enhanced problem-solving, increased resilience, improved student outcomes, and a cultural influence that extended to other institutions.

Beyond the Building

Elena's approach began influencing the broader district as other principals noticed the positive changes in her school's culture. She was invited to share her methods at conferences and professional development sessions. Most importantly, the students who experienced this conflict-positive environment carried those skills into their families and future workplaces.

The ripple effects extended far beyond what could be easily measured, contributing to a broader cultural shift toward more empathic and collaborative ways of navigating disagreement and change.

Conclusion: The Alchemy of Transformation

Elena Martinez's journey illustrates how the four-step principles used to heal individual nervous systems can also transform entire institutions. Her transition from managing division to cultivating a conflict-positive culture demonstrates the exponential power of the MindSet model when applied at the organizational level.

Elena's story reveals the complex alchemy required for cultural transformation. Individual mastery reaches its fullest potential only when supported by systematic changes in policies, structures, and norms. Her three leadership pillars created the conditions for

MindSet principles to take root and flourish as the foundation of institutional identity.

Research supports what Elena discovered: organizations that leverage disagreement as a source of creativity consistently outperform those that suppress conflict. Her faculty's transformation from philosophical division to collaborative innovation exemplifies the shift from transactional approaches to truly transformative leadership.

Elena's legacy is not one of eliminating disagreement but of transforming how her community engages with inevitable tensions. Her daily choice to see conflict as an opportunity shows that transformation is not a one-time event but a continuous practice—renewed with each encounter, deepened with each relationship, and expanded with each choice to honor the humanity in ourselves and others.

The journey from individual neurobiological awareness to organizational cultural transformation represents the highest form of crisis leadership. It requires the courage to embrace discomfort, the wisdom to recognize growth hidden within conflict, and the faith that prioritizing connection over control unlocks possibilities far beyond any single perspective.

As we prepare to explore the final chapter on personal application and commitment, Elena's story reminds us that the choice between transformation and stagnation, connection and control, hope and fear, is always before us. The tools exist. The knowledge is available. The research offers guidance. What remains is our willingness to live these principles not just during times of crisis, but as the foundation for how we choose to be with one another every day.

Transforming Organizational Culture

Achieve Transformation

Successfully reshape organizational culture to embrace conflict as a positive force.

Build Resilience

Strengthen relationships and adaptive capacity to navigate future challenges.

Implement Strategies

Apply structured approaches to foster constructive engagement and resolution.

Develop Competencies

Enhance skills in emotional intelligence and communication to manage conflict effectively.

Understand Perspectives

Explore diverse viewpoints to gain a deeper understanding of the conflict.

Recognize Conflict

Identify and acknowledge conflict as a potential catalyst for growth.

Questions for Personal Reflection or Group Discussion

Consider these questions individually or discuss them with colleagues to deepen your understanding of how transformative principles can scale to create organizational change.

Understanding Leadership in Conflict

1. **Your Leadership Philosophy** Reflect on how you typically approach conflict in leadership situations. Do you tend to avoid it, manage it, or engage productively with disagreement? How might viewing conflict as a form of organizational intelligence shift your mindset and leadership approach?
2. **Modeling Transformation** Consider how you currently model the four-step principles in your leadership interactions. Where do you see opportunities to more consistently demonstrate acknowledgment, acceptance, validation, and empowerment within your team?

Application to Your Practice

3. **Creating Psychological Safety** Consider your role in creating conditions where others feel safe to disagree, challenge ideas, or admit mistakes. What specific actions do you take to build psychological safety? What barriers might you inadvertently create?

4. **Conflict as Innovation** Reflect on a recent disagreement or tension in your organization. How might this conflict contain valuable information about needed changes or improvements? How could productive engagement with this tension lead to better solutions?

Systemic Reflection

5. **Cultural Transformation** Evaluate your organization's current relationship with conflict and disagreement. What would it look like to systematically build capacity for productive conflict across all levels? What structural changes would support this transformation?

Integration Practice

Identify one area of ongoing tension or disagreement in your organization. This week, experiment with approaching it as a source of valuable information rather than a problem to solve. Notice what insights emerge when you engage the conflict with curiosity rather than control.

References

Brown, B. (2018). *Dare to lead: Brave work, tough conversations, whole hearts*. Random House.

Deutsch, M. (1973). *The resolution of conflict: Constructive and destructive processes*. Yale University Press.

DuFour, R. (2004). What is a "professional learning community"? *Educational Leadership*, 61(8), 6-11.

Edmondson, A. C. (2019). *The fearless organization: Creating psychological safety for learning, innovation, and growth*. John Wiley & Sons.

Gadamer, H.-G. (2013). *Truth and method*. Bloomsbury Academic. (Original work published 1960)

Gee, J. P. (2015). *Social linguistics and literacies: Ideology in discourses* (5th ed.). Routledge.

Goleman, D. (1995). *Emotional intelligence: Why it matters more than IQ*. Bantam Books.

Heifetz, R. A., & Linsky, M. (2017). *Leadership on the line: Staying alive through the dangers of change* (Rev. ed.). Harvard Business Review Press.

Jehn, K. A., & Mannix, E. A. (2001). The dynamic nature of conflict: A longitudinal study of intragroup conflict and group performance. *Academy of Management Journal*, 44(2), 238-251.

Johnson, B. (2020). *Polarity management: Identifying and managing unsolvable problems* (Rev. ed.). HRD Press.

Lieberman, M. D. (2013). *Social: Why our brains are wired to connect*. Crown Publishers.

Martin, R. L. (2017). *Creating great choices: A leader's guide to integrative thinking*. Harvard Business Review Press.

Nemeth, C. J. (2012). *In defense of troublemakers: The power of dissent in life and business*. Basic Books.

Raelin, J. A. (2003). *Creating leaderful organizations: How to bring out leadership in everyone*. Berrett-Koehler Publishers.

Senge, P. M. (2006). *The fifth discipline: The art and practice of the learning organization* (Rev. ed.). Doubleday.

Chapter 9: From Understanding to Action - Your Transformative Journey

As we reach the conclusion of our exploration together, it's worth pausing to recognize the journey we've taken. We began with the understanding that crisis behavior does not stem from moral failing but from sophisticated neurobiological systems designed for survival. Along the way, we discovered practical tools that translate scientific insights into transformative action. We also saw how individual capacities can scale to reshape entire organizational cultures.

Yet knowledge alone has never transformed a life or healed a relationship. My own journey into these insights did not begin in academic study, but in the daily reality of working with students whose behaviors challenged everything I thought I knew about effective intervention.

I remember vividly a moment with Jamie, whose explosive outbursts regularly emptied classrooms, despite our best efforts to follow prescribed behavioral protocols. It wasn't until I abandoned the script one day—sitting quietly beside him during a meltdown instead of implementing the standard response—that I glimpsed the possibility of a different approach. The connection forged in that moment of quiet presence accomplished what weeks of carefully designed interventions had failed to achieve. This wasn't just a different technique; it was a fundamentally different way of understanding what crisis behavior actually represents.

That experience went beyond professional development. It offered a way of being in the world that honors the complexity of human experience while remaining committed to each person's inherent dignity.

The Personal Invitation: Your Unique Contribution

Understanding these principles intellectually is very different from embodying them in practice. The gap between knowledge and transformation is bridged not by more information but by consistent, mindful application in real-world situations.

Each of us brings unique strengths to this work. Some may have a natural empathic capacity that benefits from structured frameworks. Others bring analytical thinking that supports understanding of neurobiological foundations. Still others hold leadership roles with the power to influence systemic change. Whatever your starting point, the invitation is the same: become an agent of transformation within your sphere of influence.

This work is not about perfection. It's not about becoming a crisis management expert overnight. The goal is to commit to a journey of continuous growth, learning, and service to others' well-being.

Starting Tomorrow: Your First Steps

Transformation doesn't require dramatic shifts. It begins with small, daily choices that change how we respond to challenges.

Practice the Three-Breath Reset

Before entering any potentially challenging interaction—whether a difficult conversation with a colleague, a discipline moment with a child, or a conflict resolution meeting—take three intentional breaths. Use the first breath to notice any tension or reactivity in your body. Use the second breath to recall your intention to connect rather than control. Use the third breath to imagine yourself fully present and receptive to whatever emerges.

This simple practice creates space between stimulus and response, allowing you to choose your approach rather than simply reacting. Whether you're a teacher facing a classroom disruption, a parent dealing with a meltdown, or a manager navigating team conflict, these three breaths can shift your entire approach from reactive to responsive.

Implement Neutral Observation

Begin incorporating neutral observation into your daily interactions. When you notice someone showing signs of distress, practice describing what you observe without interpretation: "I notice you're speaking more quickly than usual," "I see you've moved away from the group," or "Your shoulders look tense right now."

This practice interrupts escalation patterns, demonstrates that you're paying attention, and creates space for the person to develop awareness of their internal state. The challenge lies in truly keeping it neutral—our minds want to add interpretation or jump to solutions. Learning to simply name what you see requires practice and patience with yourself.

Seek One "Yeah" Moment Daily

Commit to creating one genuine moment of connection each day with someone who seems to be struggling. Sometimes it's as simple as truly seeing someone who feels invisible, acknowledging a challenge they're facing, or offering validation for their experience.

These moments—when someone shifts from defensive posture to openness, when you can almost see their shoulders drop as they feel genuinely understood—build your skills while creating positive impacts in your immediate environment. Over time, you'll notice that people begin approaching you differently and conflicts de-escalate more quickly.

Building Your Practice: The Long-Term Journey

Deepen Your Self-Awareness

Transformative crisis management begins with understanding your own nervous system patterns. What situations activate your defensive responses? How do you return to regulation when triggered? Developing practices that support your own nervous system health—whether mindfulness, exercise, creative expression, or meaningful connection—becomes essential rather than optional.

Find Your Learning Community

Transformation happens most effectively within community. Seek out others who share your commitment to more empathic, effective ways of engaging with conflict. Share your learning, ask questions, and offer support to others who are on similar journeys.

Model New Possibilities

Every interaction becomes an opportunity to demonstrate different ways of engaging with conflict and challenge. When colleagues see you responding to difficult situations with curiosity rather than reactivity, they begin considering new possibilities for their own responses. Your modeling doesn't require perfection—your willingness to acknowledge mistakes and repair relationships often teaches more than flawless performance.

The Vision We're Creating Together

Each time you choose connection over control, you're contributing to a cultural evolution toward more humane ways of being together. We're working toward educational environments where every child experiences what it means to be truly seen and valued. We're creating workplaces where psychological safety enables innovation and collaboration. We're building communities where conflict becomes a catalyst for deeper understanding.

Perhaps most importantly, we're raising a generation of young people who understand that their nervous system responses are information rather than character judgments, who know how to seek help when struggling, and who possess tools for supporting others through difficult moments.

A Final Reflection

In a world that often feels divided and overwhelmed by conflict, your commitment to transformative crisis management becomes an act of profound hope. This work is both deeply personal and fundamentally collective. It requires courage to believe that a different way is possible—that conflict can be a doorway to growth, that our differences can serve as resources for learning, and that our shared humanity can ground us as we navigate even the most complex challenges.

The world needs what you have to offer. The journey continues with each breath you take, each choice you make, each person you encounter. In choosing the path of connection over control, of understanding over judgment, of empathy over indifference, you join a movement of healers working to create the world we all deserve—a world where every person experiences what it means to be truly seen, understood, and valued.

Questions for Personal Reflection or Group Discussion

Consider these questions individually or with colleagues to help integrate and apply the insights from our journey together.

Integration and Commitment

Your Transformation Journey

Reflect on how your understanding of crisis and conflict has evolved throughout this experience. What insights have been most meaningful to you? How has your response to challenging situations already begun to shift?

1. **Personal Application**

   Think about the three suggested practices: the three-breath reset, neutral observation, and seeking "yeah" moments. Which one feels most natural for you? Which feels most difficult? How will you begin incorporating these into your daily routines?

Sustaining Your Practice

3. **Support Systems** What support do you need to sustain this journey over time? Who in your life might join you in exploring these approaches? How will you continue learning and growing in your capacity for transformative crisis management?
4. **Overcoming Obstacles** What barriers do you anticipate—internal triggers, external pressures, systemic constraints? How might you prepare for these challenges while maintaining your commitment to connection over control?

Expanding Your Impact

5. **Vision for Change**

   Imagine your workplace, family, or community five years from now if these principles were widely practiced. What would look and feel different? What role do you hope to play in bringing about that transformation?

Integration Practice

This week, write a letter to yourself describing your commitment to this journey. Include specific actions you plan to take, the vision that inspires you, and reminders to help you stay grounded when the path gets hard. Seal the letter and plan to open it in six months as a personal check-in with your growth and ongoing commitment.

References

Brown, B. (2018). *Brave Work, Tough Conversations, Whole Hearts*. Random House Business.

Dana, D. (2018). *The polyvagal theory in therapy: Engaging the rhythm of regulation*. W. W. Norton & Company.

Edmondson, A. C. (2018). *The fearless organization: Creating psychological safety in the workplace for learning, innovation, and growth*. John Wiley & Sons.

Perry, B. D., & Winfrey, O. (2021). What happened to you?: Conversations on trauma, resilience, and healing. Flatiron Books.

Porges, S. W. (2011). *The polyvagal theory: Neurophysiological foundations of emotions, attachment, communication, and self-regulation*. W. W. Norton & Company.

Schore, A. N. (2003). *Affect dysregulation and disorders of the self*. W. W. Norton & Company.

Siegel, D. J. (2012). *The developing mind: How relationships and the brain interact to shape who we are* (2nd ed.). Guilford Press.

van der Kolk, B. (2014). *The body keeps the score: Brain, mind, and body in the healing of trauma*. Viking.

Made in the USA
Coppell, TX
15 February 2026

72014025R20134